ABUL A'LĀ MAWDŪDĪ

مبادیء الاسلام

«باللغة الانجليزية»

TOWARDS
UNDERSTANDING
ISLAM

Translated and edited by Khurshid Ahmad

© Islamic Foundation 1980/1400 A.H.

New revised edition.

Reprinted 1981 and 1985

ISBN 0 86037 053 4 (Paperback)
ISBN 0 86037 065 8 (Hardback)

Published by
The Islamic Foundation,
223 London Road,
Leicester LE2 1ZE, UNITED KINGDOM.

Reprinted in 1990
Sponsored by
ISLAMIC DAWAH GUIDANCE CENTER
Dammam Office
Dammam 31131
Tel. : 898-744
SAUDI ARABIA

CONTENTS

FOREWORD

Some may think it pretentious of me to write a foreword to a book by an Islamic thinker as outstanding in our time as Mawlānā Mawdūdī, especially when any need to introduce the eminent author or his remarkable book *Towards Understanding Islam* has been magisterially fulfilled by Brother Khurshid Ahmad. *Towards Understanding Islam* has already made its mark and this edition is only an improved English version. However, I can hardly neglect this opportunity to express our gratitude to Allah, *subḥānahū wata'ālā* for having enabled us to bring out a new revised version of a book which has so deeply influenced such a large number of men and women. Only recently I received a letter from a friend in Brazil, saying how a leading journalist had embraced Islam purely because of the simple and persuasive exposition of the Islamic way of life in *Towards Understanding Islam*. There must be innumerable other examples of a similar kind and I hope that the book will be even more effective in its present form.

The Islamic Foundation envisages a comprehensive plan to bring the moving and inspiring work of Mawlānā Mawdūdī before the world at large, in English and other major European languages. *Towards Understanding Islam* is only the first step and we hope that other important books by him, certainly some of the most influential in our age, will soon find their way to thirsty souls and hungry intellects.

We pray to Allah to bless our effort with mercy and acceptance.

13 December, 1979   **K. J. Murad**
24 Muḥarram 1400 A.H.   Director General

5

AUTHOR'S PREFACE
TO SECOND EDITION

The present edition of *Towards Understanding Islam* is more than a new translation of my book *Risālah Dīniyāt:* it is an entirely new and revised version. The first edition, which was rendered into English by the late Dr. Abdul Ghani (Director of Public Instruction, Afghanistan), was very brief and sketchy. Unfortunately, Dr. Abdul Ghani did not live to improve the translation. I later revised the original book and made substantial additions to it. This revised edition of *Risālah Dīniyāt* has now been skilfully translated by Prof. Khurshid Ahmad, to whom my heartfelt thanks are due for this labour of love. I am confident that the book will serve its purpose better in this new form.

My object in writing this book has been to provide all those — Muslims and non-Muslims alike — who have no access to the original sources with a brief treatise giving a lucid, comprehensive and all-embracing view of Islam. I have avoided minute details and endeavoured to portray Islam as a whole in a single perspective. Apart from stating what we Muslims believe in and stand for, I have also tried to explain the rational bases of our beliefs. Similarly, in presenting the Islamic modes of worship and the outlines of the Islamic way of life, I have also tried to unveil the wisdom behind them. I hope this small treatise will go far towards satisfying the intellectual cravings of Muslim youth, and that it will help non-Muslims to understand our real position.

Lahore   ABUL A'LĀ
11th September, 1960

7

EDITOR'S INTRODUCTION

It is a cherished intellectual fashion of our times to highlight the challenge of secular civilization to faith and religion. There is, however, very little reflection on the challenge that religion — particularly Islam — poses to the sensate culture of the age.

For the last few centuries religion in the West has been on the defensive, most often apologetic, at all times making concessions to and compromises with an approach to life and culture that is alien to the values and ideals of religion. The Muslim World has also weathered the global onslaughts of Western civilization, especially its politico-economic arm, imperialism, which inflicted many a dent and deformity. The religious approach to life and its problems was discarded and the role of religion in the socio-economic spheres became minimal. At both the conceptual and operational levels the faith and religion of all those under colonial rule, and of the Muslims in particular, was reduced to a secondary position, if not to one of total irrelevance. The situation is now changing. The tide of imperialism has receded. The Muslim World, after attaining political independence, is now engaged in an ideological effort to rediscover its cultural personality. By drawing upon its own spiritual and historical sources it is trying to develop new attitudes and roles for restructuring its own society and for the establishment of a new world order. This new resilience in the Muslim World symbolises the revivalist movement of Islam.

The Muslims look upon the crisis of the twentieth century as a crisis of values and believe that the way out of the human predicament lies in the construction of a new social order. The real need is not to seek concessions here and there or to effect a few changes in the institutional superstructures. What is needed is a searching re-examination of the foundations on which the entire structure of society is built and of the ideals which the culture aspires to achieve. The crisis in economic and political relations is the natural outcome of the ideals, values and institutions that characterize modern civilization. Islam, therefore, suggests that it is only through summoning mankind towards a new vision of man and society that its house can be set in order. This calls for a basic change in man's approach. It is only through a thorough understanding of the social ideals and values of religion and a realistic assessment of their socio-economic situation — resources, problems and constraints — that faith-oriented communities can develop a creative and innovative approach to the challenges confronting humanity today.

This approach must be ideological. The real objective which inspires the Muslims is not a package of economic and political concessions nor even certain changes in the economic superstructure, but the construction of a new world order, with its own framework of ideals, values and foundations.

The Western approach has always assumed that radical change can be brought about by changing the environment. That is why emphasis has always been placed on change in structure. This approach has failed to produce proper results. It has ignored the need to bring about change within men and women themselves and has concentrated on change in the outside world. What is needed, however, is a total change — within people themselves as well as in their social environment. The problem is not merely structural, although structural arrangements would also have to be remodelled. But the starting point must be the hearts and souls of men and women, their perception of reality and of their own place and mission in life. The Islamic approach to social change takes full cognizance of these aspects.

Islam is an Arabic word. It is derived from two root-words: one *Salm*, meaning peace and the other *Silm*, meaning submission. Islam stands for "a commitment to surrender one's will to the Will of God" and thus to be at peace with the Creator and with all that has been created by Him. It is through submission to the Will of God that peace is brought about. Harmonization of man's will with the Will of God leads to the harmonization of different spheres of life under an all-embracing ideal. Departmentalization of life into different water-tight compartments, religious and secular, sacred and profane, spiritual and material, is ruled out. There is unity of life and unity of the source of guidance. As God is One and Indivisible, so is life and our human personality. Each aspect of life is inseparable from the other. Religious and secular are not two autonomous categories; they represent two sides of the same coin. Each and every act becomes related to God and His guidance. Every human activity is given a transcendent dimension; it becomes sacred and meaningful and goal-centred.

Islam is a worldview and an outlook on life. It is based on the recognition of the unity of the Creator and of our submission to His will. Everything originates from the One God, and everyone is ultimately responsible to Him. Thus the unity of the Creator has as its corollary the Oneness of His

10

creation. Distinctions of race, colour, caste, wealth and power disappear; our relation with other persons assumes total equality by virtue of the common Creator. Henceforth our mission becomes a dedication to our Creator; worship and obedience to the Creator becomes our purpose in life.

The Creator has not left us without guidance for the conduct of our life. Ever since the beginning of creation He has sent down Prophets who have conveyed His message to humanity. They are the source from which to discover God's Will. Thus we have the chain of Prophets beginning with Adam (peace be upon him) and ending with Muḥammad (peace be upon him). Abraham, Moses, Noah, John, Zechariah and Jesus (peace be upon them) all belong to this golden chain of Prophets. The Prophets David, Moses, Jesus and Muḥammad (may peace be upon them all), brought revealed books of guidance with them. The Qur'ān, the Book revealed to the Prophet Muḥammad (peace be upon him), is the last and final of these books of guidance.

The Qur'ān contains the word of God. In it is preserved the divine revelation, unalloyed by human interpolation of any kind, unaffected by any change or loss to the original. In it is distilled the essence of all the messages sent down in the past. In it is embodied a framework for the conduct of the whole of human life. There are explicit criteria for judging between right and wrong; there are principles of individual and collective conduct. In it are depicted the human follies of the past. In it are warnings for humankind, and in it are assurances for continued guidance for those who seek God's help.

The Qur'ān has depicted a path, the Straight Path (Ṣirāṭ al-Mustaqīm), which when followed revolutionizes the whole of life. It brings about a transformation in character and galvanizes us into action. This action takes the form of purification of the self, and then unceasing effort to establish the laws of God on earth, resulting in a new order based on truth, justice, virtue and goodness.

Men and women play a crucial role in the making of this world. They act as God's vicegerents (Khulafā')—His deputies and representatives on earth. They are morally prepared to play this role. Success lies in playing it properly, by enjoining what is right and forbidding what is wrong, by freeing people from the bondage of others, by demonstrating that a sound and serene society can only result if one harmonizes one's will with the Will of God. This makes seeking the Creator's pleasure one's purpose in life, treating the whole of creation as one's partner, raising the concept of human

11

welfare from the level of mere animal needs to seeking what is best in this world and what is best in the Hereafter.

This is the Islamic worldview, and its concept of men and women and their destiny. Islam is not a religion in the Western understanding of the word. It is at once a faith and a way of life, a religion and a social order, a doctrine and a code of conduct, a set of values and principles and a social movement to realize them in history.

The uniqueness of Islamic culture lies in its values and principles. When Muslims, after an illustrious historical career, became oblivious of this fact and became obsessed with the manifestations of their culture, as against its sources, they could not even fully protect the house they had built. The strength of Islam lies in its ideals, values and principles, and their relevance to us is as great today as it has ever been in history. The message is timeless and the principles Islam embodies are of universal application.

In our search for a new world order today, Islam emphasizes that we must aspire to a new system of life through which to approach human problems from a different perspective, not merely from the perspective of limited national or regional interest, but from the perspective of what is right and wrong, and how best we can strive to evolve a just and a humane world order at different levels of our existence, individual, national and international.

That the present order is characterized by injustice and exploitation is proved beyond any shadow of doubt. But Islam suggests that the present order fails because it is based upon a wrong concept of man and of his relationship with other human beings, with society, with nature, and with the world. The search for a new order brings us to the need for a new concept of man and his role. From the viewpoint of world religions in general, and of Islam in particular, the focus of the discussion must be shifted to a new vision of man and society, to an effort to bring about change at the level of human consciousness, of values, leading to new cultural transformation.

This is the concept of Islam that lies at the root of the contemporary resurgence of Islam. It is in the framework of these parameters that the Muslims are today awakening to a new world role, facing the problems of modernization, challenging the secular concepts and institutions of the world establishment, purging their thought and society of alien intrusions

12

from Western civilization, and harnessing their resources to build a new order at home which could act as a window on the Islamic order for all humankind. Amongst the chief architects of this new awakening in the world of Islam is Mawlana Sayyid Abul A'lā Mawdūdī.

Born in 1903 C.E., Mawdūdī started his public career as early as 1918. He wrote and spoke as editor, scholar, religious thinker and leader of a movement, authoring over a hundred works of varying size and delivering more than a thousand speeches. His death in September 1979 marks the end of an era.

He made his debut in the intellectual life of the Indo-Pakistan subcontinent in 1927, at the early age of twenty-four, and created a stir by his voluminous scholarly work *Al-Jihād fi al-Islām* ("Jihad in Islam") first serialized in a newspaper, and subsequently published in the form of a book in 1930. From the early thirties he was a major, dominating, undaunted figure on the intellectual scene of the Indo-Pakistan subcontinent. The monthly magazine *Tarjumān al-Qur'ān*, which he edited since 1933, has been a major influence on the minds of the Muslim intellectuals of the subcontinent. Since the forties, when Mawlānā Mawdūdī's writings began to be available in translated versions, especially in Arabic and English, his ideas have attracted an increasing number of people far beyond the confines of the subcontinent. It is no exaggeration to say that by the time of his death he had become the most widely read Muslim author of our time, contributing immensely to the contemporary resurgence of Islamic ideas, feelings and activity all over the world.

Islam, however, was never a merely intellectual concern of Mawlānā Mawdūdī. He consciously tried to live Islam and to live for Islam. As far back as his mid-twenties he had resolved not only to devote all his energy to expounding the teachings of Islam, but also to do all that lay in his power to transform Islamic teachings into practical realities. Mawlānā Mawdūdī was always emphatic in asserting that Islam is not merely a body of metaphysical doctrines, nor merely a bundle of rituals, nor even merely a set of rules of individual conduct. It is indeed a way of life, the bases of which lie rooted in Divine Revelation; a way of life which is permeated with God-consciousness and is oriented to doing God's Will and actualising good and righteousness in human life. A Muslim is committed to follow this way of life, to bear witness to it by word and deed, and to strive in order to make it prevail in the world. Hence, in addition to his intellectual contribution, in 1941 Mawlānā Mawdūdī founded a movement known as the *Jamā'at-i Islāmī* ("The Islamic Organization"). He led this movement as its chief from

13

its inception till 1972. Even after getting himself relieved of the duties of its formal headship for reasons of health, he continued to be a major source of guidance and inspiration for those associated with the *Jamā'at-i Islāmī,* and indeed for a very large number of men and women across the globe, who do not have any affiliation to that organization. More and more people, particularly Muslims of the younger generation, are coming to appreciate Mawdūdī and even identify with the vision of Islam that he articulated so lucidly and incisively.

Mawlānā Mawdūdī, therefore, was no mere academician; he was also a man of action engaged in a grim struggle for the implementation of the Islamic vision. During this struggle the many sterling qualities of his character came to the surface — notably his magnanimity and tolerance. It is because of his involvement in practical matters, especially since 1948, that Mawlānā Mawdūdī often had to suffer persecution at the hands of the men of authority in Pakistan who failed to perceive the real motives and true character of his movement. Many a time he had to court imprisonment, not unlike some of the great heroes of Islam — Abū Ḥanīfah, Aḥmad ibn Ḥanbal, Ibn Taymīyah, Shaykh Aḥmad Sirhindī, and Sayyid Quṭb of our own time, to name only a few luminaries. Not only that, in 1953 he narrowly escaped the gallows and, in 1963, the bullets of an assassin. In braving persecution for the sake of his cause, Mawlānā Mawdūdī displayed a serene dignity and heroic fearlessness which won him the abiding love and respect of friends and foe alike.

It is remarkable that despite the exacting tasks laid on Mawlānā Mawdūdī's shoulders as the head of a large movement, he remained prolific as a writer and his writings remained impressive, not only qualitatively, but also quantitatively. His *magnum opus,* of course, is his translation and *tafsīr* (exegesis) of the Holy Qur'ān, an epitome of his elegant literary style, his erudition, and the clarity and brilliance of his thought. One of the major characteristics of Mawlānā Mawdūdī was his ability to bring out the relevance of Islam to the problems and concerns of man in the present age. This is largely because he combined with his Islamic scholarship an awareness and knowledge of the intellectual trends and practical problems of man in the modern age. In encountering the challenge of modernity, Mawlānā Mawdūdī displayed neither ultra-conservative rigidity, nor proneness to be overawed by the ideas and institutions current in our time simply because they were fashionable in the modern age or had gained respectability among the nations which are currently the leaders of the world. He wanted the Muslims to appropriate creatively the healthy and beneficial elements from the cumulative treasure of human experience, and

14

to employ them to serve the higher ends of life embodied in the Islamic tradition. It is this aspect of Mawlānā Mawdūdī which has attracted many, but at the same time repelled many others, particularly the ultra-conservative and the ultra-westernized elements in Muslim society.

Towards Understanding Islam is another of his important books. It is an elementary study of the basic concepts and principles of Islam. It offers a simple, understandable and unsophisticated interpretation of the meaning and message of Islam for the ordinary reader, particularly the young. It is not written in the brow-beating style of theology books, rich in awe-inspiring jargon and legal quibblings but of little help in bringing the reader into direct contact with the spirit of the faith.

Towards Understanding Islam is a religious text with a difference. It offers a simple exposition of Islam; its approach to life, the articles of its faith, its worship and prayers, and the scheme of life which it envisages. The method of exposition is steeped in the methodology of the Qur'ān. It offers in summary form the essential teachings of Islam. And as the book is primarily meant for lay readers and students no attempt is made to burden the mind of the reader with difficult or philosophic dissertations. The language and style of the author are clear, candid and rational.

Originally written in 1932 in Urdu, under the title *Risālah Dīniyāt*, the book was intended as a text-book for students of the higher classes and for the general public. It served an important need and became a popular Islamic reader. Most of the schools and colleges of the Indo-Pakistan subcontinent adopted it as a text-book in theology and made its study a part of their curricula. It has been translated into many of the world's languages, including English, Arabic, Hindi, Persian, German, French, Italian, Turkish, Portuguese, Swahili, Indonesian, Japanese, Malayalam, Tamil, Pushto, Bengali, Gujrati and Sindhi.

The first English translation appeared in 1940 (Translator: Dr. Abdul Ghani) and ran into many editions. In the early fifties the need for a new translation was felt for more than one reason. The earlier translation suffered from certain deficiencies. Moreover, the author re-edited the text in the forties, making substantial alterations and revisions. I was assigned the task of rendering a new translation based on the revised text (sixteenth [revised] edition), which I accomplished in the mid-fifties. Although I kept the earlier translation before me, only a very few paragraphs were finally embodied in the new translation. Strictly speaking, I did not venture a literal, word-for-word, translation of the original text. I tried to follow the

15

original as faithfully as possible, but departed wherever necessary from a strictly literal rendering in the interest of a more effective communication of the meaning of the text. The learned author was kind enough to go through my translation in 1959 and it was offered to the public with his approval.

During the last two decades many reprints of the 1959 edition have appeared. As the years went by I came to feel that the translation needed further improvement. My long stay in the United Kingdom (1968–78) provided me with an opportunity for further reflection upon a work done in my student days. Now a revised translation is being published by the Islamic Foundation. I am grateful to my friend Paul Moorman, Editor, *Middle East Education* and a former Foreign Editor, *The Times Higher Educational Supplement*, for his meticulous assistance in revising the present text. I would also like to place on record the assistance I received from Khwaja Abdul Wahid and Ansar Azam in preparing my first translation. I cannot but record my profound debt to Mawlānā Mawdūdī for the influence his ideas and his noble example have had on my own life, in all phases of its development so far, and how impoverished I feel by his departure from our midst towards life-eternal. May Allah bless his soul and enable his intellectual progeny, to which I among others feel proud to belong, to continue his mission. *Towards Understanding Islam* is one of those books which have changed the lives of many and set them along the Islamic path. Over a million copies of this book have appeared in different languages of the world. It is a unique privilege to be associated with the production of this edition of the book.

Institute of Policy Studies,   **KHURSHID AHMAD**
Islamabad, Pakistan.

1st Muḥarram, 1400
November 20, 1979.

Chapter One

THE MEANING OF ISLAM

Every religion of the world has been named either after its founder or after the community or nation in which it was born. For instance, Christianity takes its name from its prophet Jesus Christ; Buddhism from its founder, Gautama Buddha; Zoroastrianism from its founder Zoroaster; and Judaism, the religion of the Jews, from the name of the tribe Judah (of the country of Judea) where it originated. The same is true of all other religions except Islam, which enjoys the unique distinction of having no such association with any particular person or people or country. Nor is it the product of any human mind. It is a universal religion and its objective is to create and cultivate in man the quality and attitude of Islam.

Islam, in fact, is an attributive title. Anyone who possesses this attribute, whatever race, community, country or group he belongs to, is a Muslim. According to the Qur'ān (the Holy Book of the Muslims), among every people and in all ages there have been good and righteous people who possessed this attribute — and all of them were and are Muslims.

Islam — What Does it Mean?
Islam is an Arabic word and connotes submission, surrender and obedience. As a religion, Islam stands for complete submission and obedience to Allah.[1]

Everyone can see that we live in an orderly universe, where everything is assigned a place in a grand scheme. The moon, the stars and all the heavenly bodies are knit together in a magnificent system. They follow unalterable laws and make not even the slightest deviation from their ordained courses. Similarly, everything in the world, from the minute whirling electron to the mighty nebulae, invariably follows its own laws. Matter, energy and life — all obey their laws and grow and change and live and die in accordance with those laws. Even in the human world the laws of nature are paramount. Man's birth, growth and life are all regulated

---

1. Another literal meaning of the word Islam is 'peace' and this signifies that one can achieve real peace of body and mind only through submission and obedience to Allah. Such a life of obedience brings with it peace of the heart and establishes real peace in society at large. - - *Editor.*

by a set of biological laws. He derives sustenance from nature in accordance with an unalterable law. All the organs of his body, from the smallest tissues to the heart and the brain, are governed by the laws prescribed for them. In short, ours is a law-governed universe and everything in it is following the course that has been ordained for it.

This powerful, all-pervasive law, which governs all that comprises the universe, from the tiniest specks of dust to the magnificent galaxies of the heavens, is the law of God, the Creator and Ruler of the universe. As the whole of creation obeys the law of God, the whole universe, therefore, literally follows the religion of Islam — for Islam signifies nothing but obedience and submission to Allah, the Lord of the Universe. The sun, the moon, the earth and all other heavenly bodies are thus 'Muslim'. So are the air, water, heat, stones, trees and animals. Everything in the universe is 'Muslim' for it obeys God by submission to His laws. Even a man who refuses to believe in God, or offers his worship to someone other than Allah, has necessarily to be a 'Muslim' as far as his existence is concerned.

For his entire life, from the embryonic stage to the body's dissolution into dust after death, every tissue of his muscles and every limb of his body follows the course prescribed by God's law. His very tongue which, on account of his ignorance advocates the denial of God or professes multiple deities, is in its very nature 'Muslim'. His head which he wantonly bows to others besides Allah is born 'Muslim'. His heart, which, through his lack of true knowledge, cherishes love and reverence for others, is 'Muslim' by intuition. These are all obedient to the Divine Law, and their functions and movements are governed by the injunctions of that law alone.

Let us now examine the situation from a different angle. Man is so constituted that there are two distinct spheres of his activity. One is the sphere in which he finds himself totally regulated by the Divine Law. Like other creatures, he is completely caught in the grip of the physical laws of nature and is bound to follow them. But there is another sphere of his activity. He has been endowed with reason and intellect. He has the power to think and form judgements, to choose and reject, to approve and spurn. He is free to adopt whatever course of life he chooses. He can embrace any faith, and live by any ideology he likes. He may prepare his own code of conduct or accept one formulated by others. Unlike other creatures, he has been given freedom of thought, choice and action. In short, man has been bestowed with free will.

Both these aspects co-exist side by side in man's life.

In the first he, like all other creatures, is a born Muslim, invariably obeying the injunctions of God, and is bound to remain one. As far as the second aspect is concerned, he is free to become or not to become a Muslim. It is the way a person exercises this freedom which divides mankind into two groups: believers and non-believers. An individual who chooses to acknowledge his Creator, accepts Him as his real Master, honestly and scrupulously submits to His laws and injunctions and follows the code. He has achieved completeness in his Islam by consciously deciding to obey God in the domain in which he was endowed with freedom of choice. He is a perfect Muslim: his submission of his entire self to the will of Allah is Islam and nothing but Islam.

He has now consciously submitted to Him Whom he had already been unconsciously obeying. He has now willingly offered obedience to the Master Whom he already owed obedience to involuntarily. His knowledge is now real for he has acknowledged the Being Who endowed him with the power to learn and to know. Now his reason and judgement are set on an even keel — for he has rightly decided to obey the Being Who bestowed upon him the faculty of thinking and judging. His tongue is also truthful for it expresses its belief in the Lord Who gave it the faculty of speech. Now the whole of his existence is an embodiment of truth for, in all spheres of life, he voluntarily as well as involuntarily obeys the laws of One God — the Lord of the Universe. Now he is at peace with the whole universe for he worships Him Whom the whole universe worships. Such a man is God's vice-regent on earth. The whole world is for him and he is for God.

The Nature of Disbelief
In contrast to the man described above, there is the man who, although a born Muslim and unconsciously remaining one throughout his life, does not exercise his faculties of reason, intellect and intuition to recognise his Lord and Creator and misuses his freedom of choice by *choosing* to deny Him. Such a man becomes an unbeliever — in the language of Islam a *Kāfir*.

Kufr literally means 'to cover' or 'to conceal'. The man who denies God is called *Kāfir* (concealer) because he conceals *by his disbelief* what is inherent in his nature and embalmed in his own soul — for his nature is instinctively imbued with 'Islam'. His whole body functions in obedience to that instinct. Each and every particle of existence — living or lifeless — functions in accordance with 'Islam' and is fulfilling the duty that has been assigned to it. But the vision of this man has been blurred, his intellect has been befogged, and he is unable to see the obvious. His own nature has become concealed from his eyes and he thinks and acts in utter disregard of it. Reality becomes estranged from him and he gropes in the dark. Such is the nature of *Kufr*.

Kufr is a form of ignorance, or, rather, it *is* ignorance. What ignorance can be greater than to be ignorant of God, the Creator, the Lord of the Universe? A man observes the vast panorama of nature, the superb mechanism that is ceaselessly working, the grand design that is manifest in every aspect of creation — he observes this vast machine, but he does not know anything of its Maker and Director. He knows what a wonderful organism his body is but is unable to comprehend the Force that brought it into existence, the Engineer Who designed and produced it, the Creator Who made the unique living being out of lifeless stuff: carbon, calcium, sodium and the like. He witnesses a superb plan in the universe — but fails to see the Planner behind it. He sees great beauty and harmony in its working — but not the Creator. He observes a wonderful design in nature — but not the Designer! How can a man, who has so blinded himself to reality, approach true knowledge? How can one who has made the wrong beginning reach the right destination? He will fail to find the key to Reality. The Right Path will remain concealed for him and whatever his endeavours in science and arts, he will never be able to attain truth and wisdom. He will be groping in the darkness of ignorance.

Not only that; *Kufr* is a tyranny, the worst of all tyrannies. And what is 'tyranny'? It is an unjust use of force or power. It is when you compel a thing to act unjustly or against its true nature, its real will and its inherent attitude.

We have seen that all that is in the universe is obedient to God, the Creator. To obey, to live in accordance with His Will and His Law or (to put it more precisely) *to be a Muslim* is ingrained in the nature of things. God has given man power over these things, but it is incumbent that they should be used for the fulfilment of His Will and not otherwise. Anyone who disobeys God and resorts to *Kufr* perpetrates the greatest injustice, for he uses his powers of body and mind to rebel against the course of nature and becomes an instrument in the drama of disobedience. He bows his head before deities other than God and cherishes in his heart the love, reverence and fear of other powers in utter disregard of the instinctive urge of these organs. He uses his own powers and all those things over which he has authority against the explicit Will of God and thus establishes a reign of tyranny.

Can there be any greater injustice, tyranny and cruelty than that exhibited by this man who exploits and misuses everything under the sun and unscrupulously forces them to a course which affronts nature and justice?

Kufr is not mere tyranny; it is rebellion, ingratitude and infidelity. After all, what is the reality of man? Where do his power and authority come from? Is he himself the creator of his mind, his heart, his soul and other organs of his body — or have they been created by God? Has he himself created the universe and all that is in it — or has it been created by God? Who has harnessed all the powers and energies for the service of man — man or God? If everything has been created by God and God alone, then to whom do they belong? Who is their rightful sovereign? It is God and none else. And if God is the Creator, the Master and the Sovereign, then who would be a greater rebel than the man who uses God's creation against His injunctions — and who makes his mind think against God, harbours in his heart thoughts against Him, and uses his various faculties against the Sovereign's Will.

If a servant betrays his master you denounce him as faithless. If an officer becomes disloyal to the state you brand him as a traitor and renegade. If a person cheats his benefactor you have no hesitation in condemning him as ungrateful. But such acts cannot begin to compare to the one which the disbeliever commits by his *Kufr*. All that a man has and all that he uses for the benefit of others is a gift of God. The greatest obligation that a man owes on this earth is to his parents. But who has implanted the love of children in the parents' heart? Who endowed the mother with the will and power to nurture, nourish and feed her children? Who inspired the parents with the passion to spend everything in their possession for the well-being of their children? A little reflection would reveal that God is the greatest benefactor of man. He is his Creator, Lord, Nourisher, Sustainer, as well as King and Sovereign. So what can be greater betrayal, ingratitude, rebellion and treason than *Kufr*, through which a man denies and disobeys his real Lord and Sovereign?

Do not think that by committing *Kufr* man does or can do the least harm to Almighty God. Insignificant speck on the face of a tiny ball in this limitless universe that man is, what harm can he do to the Lord of the Universe Whose dominions are so infinitely vast that we have not yet been able to explore their boundaries even with the help of the most powerful telescope; Whose power is so great that myriads of heavenly bodies, like the Earth, the Moon, the Sun and the stars are, at His bidding, whirling like tiny balls; Whose wealth is so boundless that He is the sole Master of the whole universe; and Who provides for all and needs none to provide for Him? Man's revolt against Him can do Him no harm; on the other hand, by his disobedience, man treads the path of ruin and disgrace.

The inevitable consequence of this revolt and denial of reality is a failure in the ultimate ideals of life. Such a rebel will never find the thread of real knowledge and vision; for knowledge that fails to reveal its own Creator can reveal no truth. Such a man's intellect and reason always run astray; for reason which errs about its own Creator cannot illumine the paths of life.

Such a man will meet with failures in all the affairs of his life. His morality, his civic and social life, his struggle for livelihood and his family life, in short, his entire existence, will be unsatisfactory. He will spread confusion and disorder. He will, without the least compunction, shed blood, violate other men's rights and generally act destructively. His perverted thoughts and ambitions, his blurred vision and distorted scale of values, and his evil activities will make life bitter for him and for all around him.

Such a man destroys the calm and pose of life on earth. And in the life hereafter he will be held guilty for the crimes he committed against his nature. Every organ of his body — his brain, eyes, nose, hands and feet — will complain against the injustice and cruelty he had subjected them to. Every tissue of his being will denounce him before God Who, as the fountain of justice, will punish him as he deserves. This is the inglorious consequence of *Kufr*. It leads to the blind alleys of utter failure, both here and hereafter.

The Blessings of Islam
These are the evils and disadvantages of *Kufr*. Let us now look at some of the blessings of Islam.

You find in the world around you and in the small kingdom of your own self innumerable manifestations of God's divine power. This grand universe, which ceaselessly works with matchless order and in accordance with unalterable laws, is in itself a witness to the fact that its Designer, Creator and Governor is an Omnipotent, All-Powerful Being with infinite power, knowledge and resources, a Being of perfect wisdom, Whom nothing in the universe dares disobey. It is in the very nature of man, as it is with every other thing in this universe to obey Him.

Besides endowing man with the capacity to acquire knowledge, the faculty to think and reflect, and the ability to distinguish right from wrong, God has granted him a certain amount of freedom of will and action. In this freedom lies man's real trial; his knowledge, his wisdom, his power of discrimination and his freedom of will and action are all being tried and tested. Man has not been obliged to adopt any particular course, for by compulsion the very object of the trial would have been defeated. If in an examination you are compelled to write a certain answer to a question, the examination will be of

22

no use. Your merit can be properly judged only if you are allowed to answer the questions freely, according to your own knowledge and understanding. If your answer is correct you will succeed; if it is wrong you will fail, and your failure will bar the way to further progress.

The situation which man faces is similar. God has given him freedom of will and action so that he may choose whatever attitude in life he likes and considers proper for himself — Islam or *Kufr*.

By the correct use of his knowledge and intellect a man recognises his Creator, reposes belief in Him, and, in spite of being under no compulsion to do so, chooses the path of obedience to Him. He understands both his own nature and the laws and realities of nature itself; despite the power and freedom to adopt any course, he adopts the way of obedience and loyalty to God, the Creator. He is successful in his trial because he has used his intellect and all other faculties properly. He uses his eyes to see the reality, his ears to listen to the truth and his mind to form right opinions. He puts all his heart and soul into following the right way he has so chosen. He chooses Truth, sees the reality, and willingly and joyfully submits to his Lord and Master. He is intelligent, truthful and dutiful, for he has chosen light over darkness. Thus he has proved by his conduct that he is not only a seeker after Truth but is its knower and worshipper as well. Such a man is on the right path, and is destined to succeed in this world and in the world to come.

Such a man will always choose the right path in every field of knowledge and action. The man who knows God with all His attributes knows the beginning as well as the ultimate end of reality. He can never be led astray, for his first step is on the right path, and he is sure of the direction and destination of his journey in life. He will reflect on the secrets of the universe, and will try to fathom the mysteries of nature, but he will not lose his way in mazes of doubt and scepticism. His path being illumined with Divine Vision, his every step will be in the right direction. In science he will endeavour to learn the laws of nature and uncover the hidden treasures of the earth for the betterment of humanity. He will try his level best to explore all avenues of knowledge and power and to harness all that exists on earth and in the heavens in the interests of mankind.

At every stage of his enquiry his God-consciousness will save him from making evil and destructive uses of science and the scientific method. He will never think of himself as the master of all these objects, boasting to be the conqueror of nature, arrogating to himself godly and sovereign powers and nourishing the ambition of subverting the world, subduing the human race and establishing his supremacy over all and sundry by fair means or foul. Such an attitude of revolt and defiance can never be entertained by a Muslim scientist — only a *Kāfir* scientist can fall prey to such illusions and by submitting to them expose the entire human race to the danger of total destruction and annihilation.[2]

A Muslim scientist, on the other hand, will behave in an altogether different way. The deeper his insight into the world of science, the stronger will be his faith in God. His head will bow down before Him in gratitude. His feelings will be that as his Master has blessed him with greater power and knowledge so he must exert himself for his own good and for the good of humanity. Instead of arrogance there will be humility. Instead of power-drunkenness there will be a strong realisation of the need to serve humanity. His freedom will not be unbridled. He will be guided by the tenets of morality and Divine Revelation. Thus science will in his hands, instead of becoming an instrument of destruction, become an agency for human welfare and moral regeneration. And this is the way in which he will express his gratitude to his Master for the gifts and blessings He has bestowed on man.

Similarly, in history, economics, politics, law and other branches of arts and science, a Muslim will nowhere lag behind a *Kāfir* in the fields of inquiry and struggle, but their angles of view and consequently their *modus operandi* will be widely different. A Muslim will study every branch of knowledge in its true perspective. He will strive to arrive at the right conclusions.

In history he will draw correct lessons from the past experiences of man, and will uncover the true causes of the rise and fall of civilisations. He will try to benefit from all that was good and right in the past and will scrupulously avoid all that led to the decline and fall of nations. In politics his sole objective will be to strive for the establishment of policies where peace, justice, fraternity and goodness reign, where man is a brother of man and respects his humanity, where no exploitation or slavery is rampant, where

2. The situation which confronts modern man today is similar. Dr. Joad says: "Science has given us power fit for the gods, and to its use we bring the mentality of schoolboys and savages." The famous philosopher Bertrand Russell writes: "Broadly speaking, we are in the middle of a race between human skill as to means and human folly as to ends, every increase in the skill required to achieve them is to the bad. The human race has survived hitherto owing to ignorance and incompetence; but. given knowledge and competence combined with folly, there can be no certainty of survival. Knowledge is power, but it is power for evil just as much as for good. It follows that unless man increases in wisdom as much as in knowledge, increase of knowledge will be increase of sorrow." *(Impact of Science on Society*, pp. 120–121.)
Another leading thinker has put the paradox in these words: "We are taught to fly in the air like birds, and to swim in the water like fishes: *but how to live on the earth we do not know."* (Quoted by Joad in *Counter Attack From the East,* p. 28.)

the rights of the individual are upheld, and where the powers of the state are considered as a sacred trust from God and are used for the common welfare of all. In the field of law, the endeavour of a Muslim will be to make it the true embodiment of justice and the real protector of the rights of all — particularly of the weak. He will see that everybody gets his due share and no injustice or oppression is inflicted on anyone. He will respect the law, make others respect it, and will see that it is administered equitably.

The life of a Muslim will always be filled with godliness, piety, righteousness and truthfulness. He will live in the belief that God alone is the Master of all, that whatever he and other men possess has been given by God, that the powers he wields are only a trust from God, that the freedom he has been endowed with is not to be used indiscriminately, and that it is in his own interest to use it in accordance with God's Will. He will constantly keep in view that one day he will have to return to the Lord and submit an account of his entire life. The sense of accountability will always remain implanted in his mind and he will never behave irresponsibly.

Think of the moral excellence of the man who lives with this mental attitude — his will be a life of purity and piety and love and altruism. He will be a blessing unto mankind. His thinking will not be polluted with evil thoughts and perverted ambitions. He will abstain from seeing evil, hearing evil, and doing evil. He will guard his tongue and will never utter a word of lie. He will earn his living through just and fair means and will prefer hunger to a food acquired unfairly through exploitation or injustice. He will never be a party to any form of oppression or violation of human life and honour. He will never yield to evil, whatever the cost of defiance. He will be an embodiment of goodness and nobility and will defend right and truth even at the cost of his life. Such a man will be a power to be reckoned with. He is bound to succeed.

He will be highly honoured and respected. How can humiliation ever visit a person who is not prepared to bow his head before anyone except God the Almighty, the Sovereign of the universe? No one can be more powerful than he — for he fears none but God and seeks blessings from none but Him. What power can make him deviate from the right path? What wealth can buy his faith? What force can shape his conscience? What power can compel him to behave as he does not want to?

He will be the most wealthy. No one in the world can be richer or more independent than he — for he will live a life of austerity and contentment. He will be neither a sensualist, nor indulgent, nor greedy. He will be contented with whatever he earns fairly and honestly and however much ill-gotten wealth is heaped before him he will not even look at it. He will have peace and contentment of heart — and what can be a greater wealth than this?

He will be the most revered, popular and beloved. No one can be more lovable than he — for he lives a life of charity and benevolence. He will be just to everyone, discharge his duties honestly, and work for the good of others. People's hearts will be naturally drawn towards him.

No one can be more trustworthy than he — for he will not betray his trust, nor will he stray from righteousness: he will be true to his word, and straightforward and honest in his dealings. He will be fair and just in all his affairs, for he is sure that God is ever-present, ever-vigilant. Words fail to describe the credit and goodwill which such a man commands. Can there be anyone who will not trust him? Such is the life and character of a Muslim.

If you understand the true character of a Muslim, you will be convinced that he cannot live in humiliation, abasement or subjugation. He is bound to prevail and no power on earth can overwhelm him. For Islam inculcates in him the qualities which cannot be driven out.

And after living a respectable and honourable life on this earth, he will return to his Creator Who will shower on him the choicest of His blessings — for he will have discharged his duty ably, fulfilled his mission successfully and emerged from his trial triumphantly. He is successful in life in this world and in the hereafter will live in eternal peace, joy and bliss.

This is Islam, the natural religion of man, the religion which is not associated with any person, people, period or place. It is the way of nature, the religion of *man*. In every age, in every country and among every people, all God-knowing and truth-loving men have believed and lived this very religion. They were all Muslims, irrespective of whether they called that way Islam. Whatever its name was, it signified Islam and nothing but Islam.

Chapter Two

FAITH AND OBEDIENCE

Islam means obedience to God. And it is common sense that this obedience cannot be complete unless man knows certain basic facts of life and places firm faith in them. What are those facts? And what are the essentials which a man must know to fashion his life in accordance with the Divine Way? This we propose to discuss in the present chapter.

First of all, one should have an unshakable belief in the existence of God; without this, obedience to Him is clearly impossible.

Then, one must know the attributes of God. It is the knowledge of the attributes of God which enables man to cultivate the noblest of human qualities and to fashion his life in virtue and godliness. If a man does not know that there is One and only One God who is the Creator, the Ruler and the Sustainer of the Universe and there is none else to share with Him even a shred of Divine power and authority, he may fall prey to false gods, and offer his homage to them in search of favours.

But if he knows the divine attribute of *tawḥīd* (Oneness of God), there is no possibility of this. Similarly, if a man knows that God is Omnipresent and Omniscient and sees, hears and knows everything that we do in public or private — including our unexpressed thoughts! — then how can he afford to be disobedient to God? He will feel that he is under eternal vigil and will, therefore, behave accordingly. But he who is not aware of these attributes of God may be led, because of his ignorance, into disobedience. It is the same with all the other attributes of God.

The fact is that the qualities and attributes which a man must possess, if he wants to pursue the way of Islam, can be cultivated and developed only out of profound knowledge of the attributes of God. It is the knowledge of God's attributes which purifies a man's mind and soul, his beliefs, morals and actions. And a mere cursory acquaintance with or just an academic knowledge of these attributes is not sufficient — there must be an unflinching conviction firmly rooted in the mind and heart of man so that he may remain immune from insidious doubts and perversions.

Moreover, one must know in detail *the way of living* by following which one can seek the pleasure of God. Unless a man knows the likes and dislikes of God, how can he choose the one and reject the other? If a man has no knowledge of the Divine Law, how can he follow it? Thus a knowledge of the Divine Law and the Revealed Code of Life is essential.

But here, again, mere knowledge is not enough. Man must have full confidence and conviction that *it is the Divine Law* and that *his salvation lies in following* this code alone. For knowledge without this conviction will fail to spur man to the Right Path and he may be lost in the blind alley of disobedience.

Finally, man must also know the consequences both of belief and obedience and of disbelief and disobedience. He must know what blessings will be showered upon him if he chooses God's way and leads a life of purity, virtue and obedience. And he must also know what consequences follow if he adopts the way of disobedience and revolt. Thus, knowledge of life after death is absolutely essential for this purpose. Man must have an unwavering belief in the fact that death does not mean the end of life; that there will be resurrection and he will be brought to the highest court of justice, to be presided over by God Himself; that on the Day of Judgement complete justice will prevail; and that good deeds will be rewarded and misdeeds punished. Everybody will get his due; there will be no escape. This is bound to happen. A sense of accountability is essential for fully-fledged obedience to the Law of God.

A man who has no knowledge of the world to come many consider obedience and disobedience quite immaterial. He may think that the obedient and the disobedient will both meet a similar end: after death, both will be reduced to mere dust. With this attitude of mind, how can he be expected to submit to all the inconveniences and troubles that are inextricably associated with the life of active obedience, and avoid committing those sins which do not apparently bring him any moral or material loss in this world? With this mental attitude a man cannot acknowledge and submit to God's Law.

Nor can a man, who lacks *firm belief* in the life hereafter and in the Divine Court of Judgement, remain steadfast in the turbulent waters of life with its temptation to sin, crime and evil; for doubt and hesitancy rob a man of his will to action. You can remain consistent in your behaviour only if you are firm in your beliefs. You can whole-heartedly follow a course only if you are sure of the benefits that will accrue to you by following it and of the losses that will engulf you if you disobey it. Thus, a profound knowledge of the consequences of belief and disbelief and of the life after death is crucial.

These are the essential facts which one must know if one wants to live the life of obedience, that is, Islam.

Faith — What Does it Mean?

Faith is what we have described in the foregoing discussion as 'Knowledge and Belief'. The Arabic word *Īmān*, which we have rendered in English as faith, literally means 'to know', 'to believe' and 'to be convinced beyond the least shadow of doubt'. Faith, thus, is firm belief arising out of knowledge and conviction. And the man who *knows* and reposes unshakable belief in the Unity of God, in His Attributes, in His Law and the Revealed Guidance, and in the Divine Code of Reward and Punishment is called *Mu'min* (faithful). This faith invariably leads man to a life of obedience and submission to the Will of God. And one who lives this life of submission is known as *Muslim*.

It is therefore clear that without faith *(Īmān)* no man can be a true Muslim. It is the indispensable essential; rather, the very starting point, without which no beginning can be made. The relation of Islam to *Īmān* is the same as of a tree to its seed. As a tree cannot sprout forth without its seed, in the same way it is not possible for a man who has no belief to start with, to become a 'Muslim'. On the other hand, just as it can happen that, in spite of sowing the seed, the tree may, for many reasons, not grow, or if it does grow, its development may be impaired or retarded, in the same way, a man may have faith, but due to a number of weaknesses, he may not become a true and staunch Muslim.

From the viewpoint of Islam and *Īmān*, men may be classified into four categories:

1. Those who have firm faith — a faith that makes them whole-heartedly submit to God. They follow the way of God and devote themselves heart and soul to seeking His pleasure by doing all that He likes and by avoiding all that He dislikes. In their devotion they are even more fervent than is the common man in pursuit of wealth and glory. Such men are true Muslims.

2. Those who do have faith, who believe in God, His Law and the Day of Judgement, but whose faith is not deep and strong enough to make them totally submit to God. They are far below the rank of true Muslims, deserve punishment for their defaults and misdeeds, but are still Muslims. They are wrongdoers but not rebels. They acknowledge the Sovereign and His Law and, although they are violating the Law, they have not

revolted against the Sovereign. They admit His supremacy and their own guilt. Thus they are guilty and deserve punishment, but Muslims they remain.

3. Those who do not possess faith at all. These people refuse to acknowledge the sovereignty of God and are rebels. Even if their conduct is not bad and even if they are not spreading corruption and violence, they remain rebels and their apparent good deeds are of little value. Such men are like outlaws. Sometimes outlaws may act in accordance with the laws of the land, but this does not make them loyal and obedient citizens; in the same way the apparent good deeds of those who revolt against God cannot compensate for the gravity of the real wrongs, revolt and disobedience.

4. Those who neither possess faith nor do good deeds. They spread disorder in the world and perpetrate all kinds of violence and oppression. They are the worst of the people; for they are both rebels and wrongdoers and criminals.

The above classification of mankind shows that the real success and salvation of man depends on faith *(Īmān)*. The life of obedience *(Islām)* takes its birth from the seed of *Īmān*. This Islam of a person may be flawless or defective. But without *Īmān* there can be no Islam. Where there is no *Īmān* there is no Islam. Where there is no Islam there is *Kufr*. Its form and nature may vary, but it remains *Kufr* and nothing but *Kufr*.

How to Acquire Knowledge of God?
Now the question arises of how to acquire knowledge of and belief in God, His Attributes, His Law and the Day of Judgement?

We have already referred to the countless manifestations of God around us and in our own selves, which bear witness to the fact that there is One and only One Creator and Governor of this Universe and it is He Who controls and directs it. These manifestations reflect the divine attributes of the Creator: His great wisdom, His all-embracing knowledge, His omnipotence, His mercy, His all-sustaining power — in short His attributes can be traced everywhere in His works. But man's intellect and capacity for knowledge have erred in observing and understanding them. Some men have argued that there are two gods, others have professed belief in a trinity, and still others have succumbed to polytheism. Some have worshipped nature and others divided the Creator into the gods of rain, air, fire, life, death and so on.

Similarly, men have put forward many erroneous notions about life after death; for instance, that man is reduced to dust after death and will not rise to life again; or that man is subject to a process of continuous regeneration in this world and is punished or rewarded in future cycles of life.

Even greater difficulty arises when we come to the question of a code of living. To formulate a complete and balanced code that conforms to God's pleasure merely using human reason is an extremely difficult task. Even if a man is equipped with the highest faculties of reason and intellect and possesses matchless wisdom and experience, the chances of his formulating the correct views on existence are slight. And even if, after a lifetime of reflection, he does in fact succeed he will still lack the confidence that he has really discovered the truth and adopted the right path.

The fullest and fairest test of man's wisdom, reason and knowledge might have been to have left him to his own resources without any external guidance. But this would have meant that only those with the determination and ability to find the path of truth would find salvation. God, therefore, spared His human creatures such a hard test. Through His Grace and Benevolence He raised for mankind men from among themselves to whom He imparted the true knowledge of His attributes, revealed to them His Law and the Right Code of Living, gave them the knowledge of the meaning and purpose of life and of life after death and thus showed them the way by which man can achieve success and eternal bliss.

These chosen men are the Messengers of God — His Prophets. God has communicated knowledge and wisdom to them by means of revelation *(Waḥi)*, and the book containing the Divine Communications is called the Book of God, or the Word of God. The test of man's wisdom and intellect therefore lies in this: does he recognise God's Messengers after observing their pure and pious lives and carefully studying their noble and flawless teachings? A man of wisdom and common sense would accept instructions given by the Messengers of truth. If he denies the Messengers of God and their teachings, his denial would signify that he was devoid of the capacity to discover truth and righteousness. He would fail his test. Such a man will never be able to discover the truth about God and His Law and life after death.

Faith in the Unknown
It is an everyday experience that when you do not know a thing, you look for somebody who does know. If you get ill and you cannot treat and cure yourself, you go to a doctor and follow his instructions without question. Why? Because he is properly qualified to give medical advice, possesses experience and has treated and cured a number of patients. Similarly, in matters of law you accept whatever a legal expert says and act accordingly.

31

In educational matters you trust in your teacher. When you want to go to some place and do not know the way, you ask somebody who knows it, and follow the way he points out. In short, the course that you adopt in your day-to-day life about matters which you do not or cannot know is that you approach someone who does know about them, accept his advice and act accordingly. You make every effort to select the proper person. But from then on you accept his advice unquestioningly. This kind of belief is called "belief in the unknown" *(Īmān-bi'l-ghayb)*.

Īmān-bi'l-ghayb signifies that you get knowledge of what was not known to you from one who knows. You do not know God and His real attributes. You are not aware that His angels are directing the machinery of the whole Universe according to His orders, and that they surround you on all sides. You have not the proper knowledge of the way of life through which you can seek the pleasure of your Creator. And you are in the dark about the life to come. Such knowledge is given to you by the Prophets, who have had direct contact with the Divine Being. They are the persons whose sincerity, integrity, trustworthiness, godliness and absolute purity stand as irrevocable witnesses to the truth of their claim to knowledge. And above all, the wisdom and force of their message makes you admit that they speak the truth and deserve to be believed and followed.

This conviction of yours is *Īmān-bi'l-ghayb*. Such a truth-discerning and truth-acknowledging attitude is essential for obedience to God and for acting in accordance with His pleasure; for you have no other medium than God's Messengers for the achievement of true knowledge, and without true knowledge you cannot proceed on the path of Islam.

Chapter Three

THE PROPHETHOOD

Our discussion so far has made the following points:

1. The right course for man is to live in obedience to God, and for such a life of obedience knowledge and faith are absolutely essential; knowledge of God and His attributes, His likes and dislikes, His chosen way and the Day of Judgement; and unflinching faith in this knowledge; this is *Imān*.

2. God has graciously spared man the arduous task of acquiring this knowledge through his personal effort alone. Instead, He has revealed this knowledge to the Prophets He has chosen from amongst men and commanded them to convey the Will of God to other human beings and show them the right path. This has saved man from much great misfortune.

3. The duty of men and women is to recognise a true Prophet of God, to have faith in him and his teachings and to scrupulously obey him and follow in his footsteps. This is the road to salvation.

In this chapter we shall discuss the nature, history and other aspects of prophethood.

Prophethood: Its Nature and Necessity

God has most graciously provided man with all that he needs in this Universe. Generally every new-born child arrives in the world endowed with eyes to see, ears to hear, a nose to smell and breathe, hands to touch, feet to walk and a mind to think. All those potentialities, powers and faculties that a man needs or can need are most carefully provided and marvellously set in his tiny body. Every minute requirement is foreseen and provided for.

It is the same with the world he lives in. Everything essential for his life is provided: air, light, heat, water and so on. A child on opening his eyes, finds his food in his mother's breast. His parents love him instinctively and in their hearts has been implanted an irresistible urge to look after him, to bring him up and to sacrifice their all for his welfare.

Under the sheltering care of His system of sustenance the child grows to maturity and at every stage of his life obtains from nature all that he needs. All the material conditions of survival and growth are provided for; he finds that the whole Universe is at his service.

Furthermore, man is blessed with all those powers, capacities and faculties — physical, mental and moral — which he requires in his struggle for life. But God has not distributed these gifts equally. This would have made men totally independent of each other and would have excluded mutual care and co-operation. Thus, although mankind as a whole possesses all that is needed, between men capacities are distributed unequally and sparingly.

Some possess physical strength and prowess, others distinguish themselves for their mental talents. Some are born with a greater aptitude for arts, poetry and philosophy, some possess sharpness of tongue, others military acumen, commercial intelligence, mathematical keenness, scientific curiosity, literary observation or philosophical bent. These special aptitudes make a man distinct and enable him to grasp those intricacies which elude the common man. These insights, aptitudes and talents are the gifts of God. They are innate in the nature of those men whom God has destined to be thus distinguished. They cannot be acquired merely by education and training.

Reflection on this disposition of God's gifts also reveals that man's talents have been distributed in a marvellous way. Those capacities which are essential for the general maintenance of human culture have been endowed to most people, while extraordinary talents which are required only to a limited extent are given only to a small number. There are many soldiers, peasants, artisans and workers; but military generals, scholars, statesmen and intellectuals are comparatively few. The general rule seems to be: the higher the capacity and greater the genius, the fewer people who possess them. Supergeniuses, who leave an indelible mark on human history and whose achievements guide humanity for centuries, are fewer still.

Here we are faced with another question: do people just need specialists in the fields of law and politics, science and mathematics, engineering and mechanics, finance and economics and the like? Or do they also need men to show them the right path — the way to God and salvation? There must clearly be someone to tell man the purpose of creation and the meaning of life itself: what man himself is and why he has been created; who has provided him with all the powers and resources and why; what are the proper ends of life and how are they to be achieved; what are the proper values of life and how they can be attained.

34

Our reason refuses to accept that God, Who has provided man with even the smallest of his requirements, would not provide for this greatest and most vital need. It can never be so. *And it is not so.* While God has produced men of distinction in arts and science, He has also raised men with deep vision, pure intuition and the highest faculties to know and understand Him. To them, He revealed the way of godliness, piety and righteousness. He gave them the knowledge of the aims of life and values of morality and entrusted them with the duty to communicate Divine Revelation to other human beings. These men are the Prophets and Messengers of God.

The Prophets distinguish themselves in human society by their special aptitudes, natural bents of mind and a pious and meaningful way of life, more or less in the same way as other geniuses in art and science distinguish themselves by their extraordinary capacities and natural aptitudes. The genius in man is its own advertisement and automatically persuades others to recognise and acknowledge it.

Thus, a Prophet's mind grasps problems which defy other minds; he throws light on subjects which no one else can; he has insights into such subtle and intricate questions that no one else would have even understood after years of deep thought and meditation. Reason accepts whatever he says; the heart feels its truth; and experience of the world testifies to every word that flows from his mouth. If, however, we ourselves try to produce the same or a similar work, we inevitably meet with failure. In all affairs his attitude is that of truthfulness, straightforwardness and nobility. He never does or utters wrong, nor does he commit any evil. He always encourages virtue and righteousness, and practises himself what he preaches to others. Neither his words nor his deeds are prompted by self-interest. He suffers for the good of others, and never makes others suffer for his own good.

When it becomes quite clear that a person is a true Prophet of God, the natural dictate of this realisation is that his words should be accepted, his instructions followed and his orders obeyed. It is illogical to accept a man as God's true Prophet and yet not to believe in what he says and not to follow what he ordains; for your very acceptance of him as God's Prophet means that you have acknowledged that what he says is from God, and that whatever he does is in accordance with God's Will and Pleasure. Disobedience of him is disobedience of God — and disobedience of God leads to ruin.

Therefore, the very acceptance of a Prophet makes it incumbent on you to

35

follow his instructions unconditionally. You may not be able fully to grasp the wisdom and usefulness of this or that order, but the very fact that an instruction has emanated from a Prophet is sufficient guarantee of its truth. One's inability to understand it does not mean there is something wrong with it. Rather it is our understanding which is at fault.

Some men admit the integrity and truthfulness of a Prophet, but do not put faith *(Iman)* in him, nor do they follow him in the affairs of their life. Such men are not only *Kafirs,* but imprudent: for not to follow a Prophet after admitting him to be true means that one knowingly follows untruth. And what folly can be greater than that!

Some people declare: "We do not need a Prophet for our guidance and we can ourselves find the way to truth." This, too, is a wrong view. You have probably learnt geometry, and you know that between points there can be only one straight line; all other lines must be crooked or will fail to touch the points in view. The same is the case with the way to truth, which in the language of Islam, is called the Straight Path *(al-Ṣirāṭ al-Mustaqīm).* This path begins from man and goes straight up to God, and this path can by definition be one and only one; all other paths must be aberrations. This Straight Path has been indicated by the Prophets, and there is and can be no straight path besides that. The man who ignores that path soon finds himself lost in the maze created by his own fancy. What can you think of a person who loses his way and, when a good man shows him the right one, defiantly declares: "I will not take your guidance nor accept the way you have shown to me, but I will myself grope in this unknown region and try to reach the object of my search in my own way?" This, in the presence of the clear guidance of the Prophets, is sheer stupidity. If everybody tried to start from scratch, it would be a gross waste of time and energy. We never do so in the sciences and arts: why here?

If you go a little deeper into the matter, it will become clear that a person who disbelieves in a true Prophet cannot find any way, straight or otherwise, to God. This is because a man who refuses to believe the advice of a truthful man adopts such a perverse attitude that he ceases to understand the difference between truth and falsehood and becomes a victim of his own obstinacy, arrogance, bias and perversity. This refusal may be due to false arrogance, or blind conservatism and obstinate adherence to the way of one's forefathers, or to slavery to the lower desires of the self, whose gratification becomes impossible by submission to the teachings of the Prophets.

On the other hand, if a man is sincere and truth-loving, the road to reality opens up to him. He will find in the teachings of the Prophets the very echo of his own soul and discover himself by discovering the Prophets.

Above all, a true Prophet is raised by God Himself. It is He Who has sent him to mankind to convey His message to His people. It is His Command that one should put one's faith in the Prophet and follow him. Thus, one who refuses to believe in God's Messenger refuses to follow God's Commandment and becomes a rebel. There is no denying that one who refuses to acknowledge the authority of the viceroy of a sovereign actually refuses the authority of the sovereign himself. This disobedience turns him into a rebel. God is the Lord of the Universe, the true Sovereign, the King of Kings, and it is the bounden duty of every man to acknowledge the authority of His Messengers and Apostles and to obey them as His accredited Prophets. Anyone who rejects the Prophets of God is a *Kāfir*, be he a believer in God or a disbeliever.

Brief History of Prophethood
Now let us look at the history of prophethood. Let us see how this long chain began, how it gradually unfolded itself and finally culminated in the prophethood of the last of the Prophets, Muhammad (blessings of Allah and peace be upon him).

The human race began from one man: Adam. It was from him that the family of man grew and the human race multiplied. All human beings born in this world have descended from that earliest pair: Adam and Eve.[1] History and religion are agreed on this point. Nor do scientific investigations into the origin of man show that originally different men came into being, simultaneously or at different points of time, in different parts of the world. Most scientists conjecture that one man would have been brought into existence first and the entire human race might have descended from that one man.

Adam, the first man on earth, was also the first Prophet of God. He revealed His religion — Islam — to him and told him to convey and communicate it to his descendents: to teach them that Allah is One, the Creator, the Sustainer of the world; that He is the Lord of the Universe and He alone should be worshipped and obeyed; that to Him they would have to return one day and to Him alone they should appeal for help; that they should live righteous lives in accordance with God's pleasure and that if

---

1. This is a very important and revolutionary concept. Its logical outcome is unity of mankind and the equality of human beings. It is stupid to distinguish and discriminate between men on grounds of class, colour, race or territory. In an age when nationalism, narrow racialism and bloodthirsty anti-semitism have torn the world into shreds, this creed of the unity of mankind is a powerful ray of hope for the future. - *Editor.*

they did so they would be blessed and if they did not they would suffer both here and in the hereafter.

Those of Adam's descendants who were good trod the right path, but those who were bad abandoned their father's teachings. Some began to worship the sun, the moon and the stars; others took to the worship of trees, animals and rivers. Some believed that air, water, fire, health and all the blessings and forces of Nature were each under the control of a different god and that the favour of each one could be won by worship. In this way ignorance gave rise to many forms of polytheism and idolatry, and scores of religions were formulated. This was the age when Adam's progeny had spread over the globe, and formed different races and nations. Every nation had created a different religion for itself, each with rituals of its own. God — the one Lord and Creator of mankind and the universe — was forgotten. Every kind of evil custom grew; many evils began to be considered right and many right things were either ignored or condemned as wrong.[2]

At this stage God began to raise Prophets among every people. Each one reminded his people of the lesson they had forgotten. They put an end to idol-worship and the practice of associating other deities with God *(shirk)*, did away with all customs of ignorance, taught them the right way of living in accordance with God's pleasure, and gave them laws to be followed and enforced in society. God's true Prophets were raised in every land and among every people. They all possessed one and the same religion — the religion of Islam.[3]

No doubt the methods of teaching and the legal codes of different Prophets varied in accordance with the needs and the stage of culture of the people among whom they were raised. The particular teachings of each Prophet were determined by the kind of evils which he was trying to eradicate. When people were in the primitive stages of society, civilisation and intellectual development, their laws and regulations were simple; they were modified and improved as the society evolved and progressed.

---

2. This view of the history of religions is diametrically opposed to the so-called evolutionary view of religion which regards nature-worship as the first stage. More modern scientific studies are confirming the view that worship of one God *(Tawḥīd)* was the earliest form of worship and all other forms are perversions of that original religion. Those who want to pursue the topic may refer to Prof. W. Schmidt's valuable research treatise, *The Origin and Growth of Religions*, English translation by H. J. Rose (London, Methuen). — *Editor.*

3. There is a common misconception, mostly among Western writers, that Islam owes its origin to the Prophet Muḥammad (blessings of Allah and peace be upon him) and some of the writers even go to the extent of calling him 'the founder of Islam'. This is a travesty of the truth. Islam has been the religion of all the Prophets of God and all of them have brought the same message from Him. Prophets have not been the founders of Islam; they have only been the messengers of it. Islam consists of the Divine Revelation conveyed to mankind by the truthful Prophets. — *Editor.*

Such differences were, however, only superficial. The fundamental teachings of all the religions were the same, i.e. belief in the unity of God, adherence to a life of piety, goodness and peace, and belief in life after death with its just mechanism of reward and punishment.

Man's attitude towards God's Prophets has been strange. He has ill-treated them and refused to accept their teachings. Some of the prophets were expelled from their lands; some were assassinated; some, faced with indifference, preached the whole of their lives without winning more than a few followers. But despite the harassment, derision and indignity, to which they were perpetually subjected, these Apostles of God did not cease to spread their message. Their patient determination at last succeeded: large groups of people and nations were converted to their creed.

The false tendencies, born of centuries of deviation, ignorance and malpractice, now took another form. Though they accepted their Prophets during their lives and practised their teachings, after their deaths they introduced their own distorted ideas into their religions. They adopted novel methods of worshipping God; some even took to the worship of their Prophets. They made the Prophets the incarnations of God or the sons of God; some associated their Prophets with God in His Divinity.

In short, man's varied attitudes in this respect were a travesty of his reason and a mockery of himself; he made idols of those very persons whose holy mission was to smash idols.

By intermixing religion, rituals born of ignorance, baseless and false anecdotes and man-made laws, men so changed and perverted the teachings of the Prophets over the centuries that they became lost in a welter of fictions to the extent that it became impossible to distinguish the grain from the chaff. Not content with this, they made up so many stories about their Prophets that real and reliable accounts of their lives became impossible to discern. Despite all this, the work of the Prophets was not altogether in vain. Traces of truth survived. The idea of God and of life after death was assimilated in some form or other. A few principles of goodness, truthfulness and morality were accepted throughout the world. The prophets thus prepared the mental attitude of their respective peoples in such a way that a universal religion could be safely introduced — a religion which accords with the nature of man, which embodies all that was good in all other creeds and societies, and which is acceptable to mankind.

As we have said above, in the beginning separate Prophets appeared among different nations or groups of people, and the teaching of each Prophet was meant specially and specifically for his people. The reason was that at that stage of history, nations were so cut off from each other geographically that opportunities for mutual intercourse were non-existent. In such circumstances it was very difficult to propagate a common World Faith with an accompanying common system of law.

In addition, the ignorance of the early nations was so great that it had given different forms to their moral aberrations and distortions of Faith. It was, therefore, necessary that different Prophets be raised to preach the Truth to them and win them over to God; to gradually eradicate evils and aberrations; to root out ignorance and teach them the simple, pious and righteous life. God alone knows how many thousands of years were spent in thus educating man, and developing him mentally, morally and spiritually.

With the progress and spread of commerce, industry and the arts, intercourse was established between nations. From China and Japan, as far as the distant lands of Europe and Africa, regular routes were opened both by sea and land. Many people learnt the art of writing; knowledge spread. Ideas began to be communicated from one country to another and learning and scholarship began to be exchanged. Great conquerors appeared, extended their conquests far and wide, established vast empires, and knit many different nations under one political system. Thus nations came closer and closer to one another, and their differences became less and less.

It became possible under these circumstances that one and the same faith, envisaging a comprehensive and all-embracing way of life, meeting the moral, spiritual, social, cultural, political, economic and other needs of men and embodying both religious and secular elements could be sent by God to the whole 'of mankind. More than two thousand years ago mankind had reached such a mental awareness that it seemed to be craving for a universal religion.

Buddhism, though it consisted only of a set of moral principles and was not a complete system of life, emerged from India, and spread as far as Japan and Mongolia on one side, and Afghanistan and Bokhara on the other. Its missionaries travelled far and wide in the world. A few centuries later, Christianity appeared. Although the religion taught by Jesus Christ (peace be upon him) was pure *Islam*, his followers reduced it to a hotch-potch called Christianity, and even this overtly Israelised religion spread to far-off Persia and Asia Minor and to the distant climes of Europe and Africa. From these events it is evident that the conditions of mankind in that age demanded a common religion for the whole human race. Indeed, when people found no complete and true religion in existence they began to develop existing religions, however defective, incomplete and unsatisfying they might have been.

At such a crucial stage of human civilisation, when the mind of man was itself craving for a world religion, a Prophet was raised in Arabia for the whole world and for all nations. The religion he was given to propagate was again Islam — but now in the form of a complete and fully-fledged system, covering all aspects of the life of man. He was Muḥammad, the Prophet of Islam (blessings of Allah and peace be upon him)!

The Prophethood of Muḥammad
If we cast a glance at the world atlas, we find that no other country could have been more suitable than Arabia for the much-needed world religion. It is situated right in the middle of Asia and Africa, and Europe is not far away. At the time of Muḥammad's (blessings of Allah and peace be upon him) appearance central Europe was inhabited by civilised and culturally advanced nations; these people were about the same distance from Arabia as were the people of India.

Look at the history of that era, too, and you will find that no other people were more suited to be endowed with this Prophet than the Arabs. Great nations of the world had long been struggling for world supremacy; as a consequence they had exhausted their resources and vitality. The Arabs were a fresh and virile people. So-called social progress had produced bad habits among the advanced nations, while among the Arabs no such social organisation existed, and they were, therefore, free from the inactivity, debasement and decadence arising out of luxury and sensual satiety.

The pagan Arabs of the fifth century had not been affected by the evil influence of the artificial social systems and civilisations of the great nations of the world. They possessed all the good human qualities of a people untouched by the 'social progress' of the time. They were brave, fearless, generous, faithful to their promises, lovers of freedom and politically independent — not subject to the hegemony of any of the imperial powers.

There were also certain undesirable aspects of their life as well, as we shall mention later on, but the reason for this was that for thousands of years no prophet had risen among them, nor had there appeared a reformer who might have civilised them and purged their moral life of its impurities. Centuries of free and independent desert life had bred and nourished extreme ignorance among them. They had, therefore, become so fixed in their traditions of ignorance that to humanise them was beyond an ordinary man.

At the same time, however, if some person of extraordinary powers were to give them a noble ideal, they would readily rise to act for the achievement of such an ideal. They would be prepared to face the hostility of the entire world in the cause of their mission. It was just such a young, forceful and virile people that was needed to disseminate the teachings of the World Prophet, Muḥammad (blessings of Allah and peace be upon him).

Take also the Arabic language. The more you study its literature, the more you will be convinced that there is no other language more suited to express high ideals, to explain the most subtle aspects of Divine knowledge, and to impress the heart of man and mould it into submission to God. Small phrases and brief sentences express a whole world of ideas; they are so powerful that their very sound can move men to tears and ecstasy. They are so sweet that it is as if honey were being poured into one's ears; they are so full of harmony that every fibre of the listener's body is moved by their symphony. It was a rich and powerful language such as this that was needed for the Qur'ān, the Great Word of God.

It was, therefore, a manifestation of God's great wisdom that He chose Arabia as the birth-place of the World Prophet. Let us now see how unique and extraordinary was the blessed personality chosen by God for this mission.

Muḥammad's Prophethood: A Rational Vindication
If one were to close one's eyes and imagine oneself in the world of 1400 years ago, one would find that it was a world completely different from ours. How few and far between were the opportunities for the exchange of ideas! How limited and undeveloped were the means of communication! How meagre was man's knowledge! How narrow his outlook! How enveloped was he in superstition and wild ideas!

Darkness held sway. There was only a faint glimmer of learning, hardly strong enough to light up the horizons of human knowledge. There was neither radio nor telephone, neither television nor the cinema. Railways and cars and aeroplanes were undreamt of, and printing presses were unknown. Hand-written books or copyists alone supplied what little literary material there was to be transmitted from generation to generation. Education was a luxury, meant only for the most fortunate, and educational institutions were very few and far between.

42

The store of human knowledge was scanty, man's outlook was narrow, and his ideas of men and things were confined to his limited surroundings. Even a scholar of that age lacked in some respects the knowledge possessed by a layman of today, and the most cultured person was less refined than the modern man in the street.

Indeed, humanity was steeped in ignorance and superstition. Whatever light of learning there was seemed to be fighting a losing battle against the darkness prevailing all around. People used to spend a whole lifetime acquiring the modest information which is now everybody's heritage. Things which are classed as 'myth' and 'superstition' today were the unquestionable truths of that age. Acts which we now regard as barbarous were then the order of the day. Methods which appear obnoxious to our moral sense today constituted the very soul of morality; incredulity had assumed such proportions and had become so widespread that people refused to consider anything as sublime unless it appeared in the garb of the supernatural, the uncanny and even the impossible. They had developed such inferiority complexes that they could not imagine human beings possessing saintly souls.

Arabia — The Abyss of Darkness
In that benighted era, there was a territory where darkness lay even heavier than elsewhere. The neighbouring countries of Persia, Byzantium and Egypt possessed a glimmer of civilisation and a faint light of learning. But Arabia stood isolated, cut off by vast tracts of desert.

Arab traders travelling great distances, which took them months, carried their wares to and from these countries, but they had little chance to find out anything about them. In their own country, they did not have a single educational institution or library. No one seemed interested in the cultivation and advancement of knowledge. The few who were literate were not educated enough to understand the existing arts and sciences. Although they did possess a highly developed language capable of expressing the finest shades of human thought in a remarkable manner, a study of the remnants of their literature reveals how limited was their knowledge, how low was their standard of culture and civilisation, how saturated were their minds with superstitions, how barbarous and ferocious were their thoughts and customs, and how decadent were their moral standards.

It was a country without a government. Each tribe considered itself to be an independent sovereign unit. There was no law except the law of the strongest. Loot, arson and murder of innocent and weak people was the order of the day. Life, property and honour were constantly in jeopardy. Tribes were always at daggers drawn with one another. Any trivial incident was enough to spark off a ferocious war. Indeed, Bedouins from one tribe thought they had every right to kill people from other tribes.[4]

Whatever notions they had of morals, culture and civilisation were primitive in the extreme. They could hardly discriminate between pure and impure, lawful and unlawful. Their lives were barbaric. They revelled in adultery, gambling and drinking. Looting and murder were part of their everyday existence. They would stand stark naked before each other without any qualms of conscience. Even their women-folk would strip nude at the ceremony of circumambulating the Ka'bah. They would bury their daughters alive lest anyone should become their son-in-law. They would marry their step-mothers after the death of their fathers. They were ignorant of even the rudiments of everyday life such as proper eating, dressing and washing.

As regards their religious beliefs, they suffered from the same evils which were playing havoc with the rest of the world. They worshipped stones, trees, idols, stars and spirits; in short, everything conceivable except God.

They knew nothing about the teachings of the Prophets of old. They had an idea that Abraham and Ishmael were their forefathers, but they knew next to nothing about their religious preachings and about the God Whom they worshipped. The stories of 'Ad and Thamūd were to be found in their folklore, but they contained no traces of the teachings of the Prophets Hud and Salih. The Jews and Christians had passed on to them certain legends relating to the Israelite Prophets. They presented a harrowing picture of those noble souls. Their teachings were adulterated with the figments of their own imagination and their lives were tarred black. Some idea of the religious conceptions of those people can still be got today by looking at those Israelite traditions which Muslim commentators of the Qur'ān have conveyed to us. The picture presented of the institution of prophethood and of the character of the Israelite Prophets is the very antithesis of all that those noble followers of truth stood for.

The Saviour is Born
In such a dark age and in such a benighted country a man is born. His parents die when he is very young and a few years later the sad demise of

---

4. Prof. Joseph Hell writes in *The Arab Civilisation* (p. 10): "These struggles destroyed the sense of national unity and developed an incurable *particularism;* each tribe deeming itself self-sufficient and regarding the rest as its legitimate victims for murder, robbery and plunder."

his grandfather also occurs. Consequently, he is deprived even of that scant training and upbringing which an Arab child of his time could get. In his boyhood he tends flocks of sheep and goats in the company of Bedouin boys. When of age, he takes to commerce. All his associations and all his dealings are with the Arabs alone, whose condition has just been described.

He is completely illiterate and unschooled. He never gets a chance to sit in the company of learned men, for such men were non-existent in Arabia. He does have a few opportunities to go out of his country, but those journeys are confined to Syria and are nothing more than the usual business trips undertaken by Arab trade caravans. If he meets any learned men there, such random meetings are so rare as to play no part in the forming of his personality. Nor can they be the means of the acquisition of that profound and vast knowledge which transformed an unlettered Bedouin into a leader not only of his own country and age but of the whole world and of all ages to come. These journeys cannot have given him those conceptions and principles of religion, ethics, culture and civilisation: they were non-existent in the world of those days. And they cannot have created that sublime and perfect human character which was nowhere to be found in those days.

Diamond in a Heap of Stones
We may now look at the life and work of this noble man in the context not only of the Arabian society but also of the entire world as it stood in that period.

He is totally different from the people among whom he is born and passes his youth and early manhood and attains finally his full stature. Even his worst enemies never accuse him of telling a lie. He never uses obscene and abusive language. He has a charming personality and winning manners with which he captivates the hearts of those who come into contact with him. In his dealings with people he always follows the principles of justice and fair play. He remains engaged in trade and commerce for years, but he never enters into any dishonest transaction. Those who deal with him in business have full confidence in his integrity. The entire nation calls him *Al-Amin* (the Truthful and the Trustworthy). Even his enemies deposit their valuable belongings with him for safe custody.

He is the embodiment of modesty in the midst of a society which is immodest to the core. Born and bred among a people who regard drunkenness and gambling as virtues, he never touches alcohol and never indulges in gambling. His people are uncouth, uncultured and unclean, but he personifies the highest culture and the most refined aesthetic outlook.

Surrounded on all sides by cruelty, he himself has a heart overflowing with the milk of human kindness. He helps orphans and widows. He is hospitable to travellers. He harms no one; rather, he suffers hardships for others' sakes. Living among those for whom war is bread and butter, he is such a lover of peace that his heart melts for them when they take up arms and cut each other's throats. He stays aloof from the feuds of his tribe, intervening only to bring about reconciliation. Brought up in an idolatrous race, he regards nothing in the heavens and the earth worth worshipping except the One True God. He does not bow before any created thing and does not partake of the offerings made to idols, even in his childhood. Instinctively he hates all worship of any creature and being except God.

In brief, the towering and radiant personality of *this man,* in the midst of such a benighted and dark environment, may be likened to a beacon-light illumining a pitch-dark night or to a diamond shining in a heap of dead stones.

A Revolution Comes

After spending a great part of his life in such a pure and civilised manner there comes a revolution in his being. He has had enough of the darkness and ignorance around him. He wants to swim clear of the horrible sea of corruption, immorality, idolatry and disorder which surround him. He finds society out of harmony with his soul. He withdraws alone to the hills, spending days and nights in total seclusion and meditation. He fasts so that his soul and his heart may become still purer and nobler.

He muses and ponders deeply. He is in search of a light to melt away the encompassing darkness. He wants the power to bring about the downfall of the corrupt and disorderly world of his day and lay the foundations of a new and better world.

Suddenly his heart is illuminated with the Divine Light giving him the power he has yearned for. He comes out of the confinement of his cave, goes to the people, and addresses them thus:

"The idols which you worship are a sham. Stop worshipping them from now on. No mortal being, no star, no tree, no stone, no spirit is worthy of human worship. Therefore bow not your heads in worship before them. The entire universe with everything that it contains belongs to God Almighty. He alone is the Creator, the Nourisher, the Sustainer and, consequently, the real Sovereign before Whom all should bow down and to Whom all should pray and render obedience. Thus worship Him alone and obey only His commands.

46

"Loot and plunder, murder and rapine, injustice and cruelty — all the vices in which you indulge — are crimes in the eyes of God. Leave your evil ways. He hates them all. Speak the truth. Be just. Do not kill anyone. Do not rob anyone. Take your lawful share. Give what is due to others in a just manner.

"You are human beings and all human beings are equal in the eyes of God. None is born with the slur of shame on his face; nor has anyone come into the world with the mantle of honour hung around his neck. He alone is high and honoured who is God fearing and pious, true in words and deed. Distinctions of birth and race are no criteria of greatness and honour. One who fears God and does good deeds is the noblest of human beings. One who does not love God and is steeped in bad ways is doomed.

"There is an appointed day after your death when you shall have to appear before your Lord. You shall be called to account for all your deeds, good or bad, and you shall not be able then to hide anything. The whole record of your life shall be an open book to Him. Your fate shall be determined by your good or bad actions. In the court of the True Judge—the Omniscient God — the question of unfair recommendation and favouritism does not arise. You will not be able to bribe Him. No consideration will be given to your pedigree or parentage. *True faith and good deeds alone will stand you in good stead at that time.* He who has them shall take his abode in the Heaven of eternal happiness, while he who is devoid of them shall be cast in the fire of Hell."

This is the message with which he comes. The ignorant nation turns against him. Abuse and stones are showered on his august person. Every conceivable torture and cruelty is perpetrated on him; and this continues not for a day or two but uninterruptedly for thirteen long, troubled years. At last he is exiled. But he is not given respite even there. He is tormented in various ways in his place of refuge. The whole of Arabia is incited against him. He is persecuted and hounded continuously for fully eight years there. He suffers it all, but does not budge from the stand he has taken. He is resolute, firm and inflexible in his purpose.

Why all that Enmity?
One might ask: how is it that his nation became his sworn enemy? Was there any dispute about gold and silver or other worldly possessions? Was it due to any blood-feud? Did he ask for anything from them? No! The whole enmity was based on the fact that he had asked them to worship the One True God and to lead lives of righteousness, piety and goodness. He had

47

preached against idolatry and the worship of other beings besides God, and had denounced their way of life. He had cut at the roots of priestcraft. He had inveighed against all distinctions of high and low between human beings, and had condemned the prejudices of tribe and race as sheer ignorance; and he wanted to change the whole structure of society which had been handed down to them from time immemorial.

In their turn, his countrymen told him that the principles of his mission were hostile to their ancestral traditions and asked him either to give them up or to bear the worst consequences.

Why did he suffer all those hardships? His nation offered to accept him as their king and to lay all the riches of the land at his feet if only he would stop preaching his religion and spreading his message.[5] But he chose instead to refuse the tempting offers and to suffer for his cause.

Why? What had he to gain, if those people became pious and righteous?

Why was it that he cared nothing for riches and luxury, kingship and glory, and ease and plenty? Was he playing for some higher material gain so that these blessings sank into insignificance in comparison with them? Were those gains so tempting that he could elect to go through fire and sword and bear tortures of the soul and torments of the body with equanimity for years? One has to ponder these questions deeply to find the answer.

Can anyone imagine a higher example of self-sacrifice, fellow-feeling and humanity than that a man may ruin his own happiness for the good of others, while those very people for whose betterment he is striving should

5. The Prophet Muḥammad (blessings of Allah and peace be upon him) had to face tempests of adversity in the cause of truth. He faced all the opposition and oppression with a smile. He stood firm, undeterred by criticism and coercion. When the natives saw that the threats failed to frighten him and the severest tribulations heaped upon his person and his followers could not make them budge, they played another trick — but that too was destined to fail!
A deputation of the leading Quraish called upon the Holy Prophet and tried to bribe him by offering all the worldly glory they could imagine. They said: "If you want to possess wealth, we will amass for you as much as you wish; if you aspire to win honour and power we are prepared to swear allegiance to you as our overlord and king; if you have a fancy for beauty, you shall have the hand of the most beautiful maiden of your choice."
But they wanted him to abandon his mission. The terms were extremely tempting for any human mortal. But they had no significance for the Great Prophet. His reply fell like a bomb-shell upon the deputation: "Pray! I want neither wealth nor power. I have been commissioned by God to warn mankind. I deliver His message to you. Should you accept it, you shall have joy in this life and eternal bliss in the life hereafter; should you reject it, surely God will decide between you and me."
On another occasion he said to his uncle, who, under pressure from the leaders of Arabia, was trying to persuade him to abandon his mission: "O Uncle! Should they place the sun in my right hand and the moon in my left in order to make me renounce this mission, it would not be so. I will never give it up till it should please God to make it a triumph or I perish in the attempt."
This was the character of the Prophet of Islam! — *Editor.*

stone him, abuse him, banish him and harass him even in his exile, and that, in spite of all this, he should continue striving for their well-being?

Can anyone who is insincere undergo so much suffering for a false cause? Can anyone who is dishonest exhibit such determination to stick to his guns in the face of dangers and tortures of every description when a whole country rises up in arms against him?

The faith, perseverance and resolution with which he led his movement to ultimate success is eloquent proof of the supreme truth of his cause. Had there been the slightest doubt and uncertainty in his heart, he could never have been able to brave the storm which continued unabated for twenty-one long years.

This is one side of the revolution wrought in his being. The other is even more wonderful and remarkable.

A Changed Man at Forty — Why?
For forty years he lived as an Arab among Arabs. During that long period he was not known as a statesman, a preacher or an orator. No-one had heard him imparting gems of wisdom and knowledge as he began to do hereafter. He was never seen discoursing on metaphysics, ethics, law, politics, economics and sociology. Let alone being a great general, he was not even known as an ordinary soldier. He had uttered no word about God, the Angels, the Revealed Books, the early Prophets, the bygone nations, the Day of Judgement, Life after Death, Hell and Heaven.

Although he possessed an excellent character and charming manners, and was highly cultured, there was nothing so striking about him which could make men expect something great and revolutionary from him in the future. He was known among his acquaintances as a sober, calm, gentle, law-abiding citizen of good nature. But when he came out of the cave with his Message he was transformed.

When he began preaching his Message the whole of Arabia stood in awe and wonder and was bewitched by his wonderful eloquence and oratory. It was so impressive and persuasive that his worst enemies were afraid of hearing it, lest it should penetrate deep into their hearts or the very marrow of their beings and convert them from their old religion and culture. It was so unique that the whole legion of Arab poets, preachers and orators of the highest calibre failed to match it in beauty of language and splendour of diction when he threw the challenge to his opponents to produce even a single line like the ones he was reciting.

His All-embracing Message

Along with this, he now appeared before his people as a unique philosopher, a wonderful reformer, a renowned moulder of culture and civilisation, an illustrious politician, a great leader, a judge of the highest eminence and an incomparable general. This unlettered Bedouin, this desert dweller, spoke with learning and wisdom, the like of which none had said before and none could say after him.

He expounded the complex problems of metaphysics and theology. He delivered speeches on the decline and fall of nations and empires, supporting his thesis with historical fact. He reviewed the achievements of the old reformers, passed judgements on the various religions of the world, and gave verdicts on the differences and disputes between nations. He taught ethical canons and principles of culture. He formulated laws of social culture, economic organisation, group conduct and international relations whose wisdom even eminent thinkers and scholars can grasp only after life-long research and vast experience of men and things. Their beauties, indeed, unfold themselves progressively as man advances in theoretical knowledge and practical experience.

This silent and peace-loving trader who had never even handled a sword before turned suddenly into such a brave soldier that he was never known to retreat however fierce the battle. He became such a great general that he conquered the whole of Arabia in nine years, at a time when the weapons of war were primitive and the means of communication very poor. His military acumen and his ability to transmit the skills of war to a motley crowd of Arabs (who had no equipment worth the name) meant that within a few years he had overthrown the two most formidable military powers of the day and become the master of the greater part of the then known world.

This reserved and quiet man who, for fully forty years, never gave any indication of any political interest or activity, appeared suddenly on the stage of the world as such a great political reformer and statesman that, without the aid of the media, he brought together under one banner, one law, one religion, one culture, one civilisation and one form of government the scattered inhabitants of a desert of twelve hundred thousand square miles — a people who were warlike, ignorant, unruly, uncultured and plunged in internecine tribal warfare.[6]

---

6. Sir William Muir, a staunch critic of Islam, admits in his book, *The Life of Mohammad (p. xciv)*: "The first peculiarity, then, which attracts our attention is the subdivision of the Arabs into innumerable bodies ... each independent of the others; restless and often at war amongst themselves; and even when united by blood or by interest, ever ready on some insignificant cause to separate and give way to an implacable hostility. Thus at the era of Islám the retrospect of Arabian history exhibits, as in the kaleidoscope, an ever-varying state of combination and repulsion, such as had hitherto rendered abortive any attempt at a general union ... The problem had yet to be solved, by what force these tribes could be subdued, or drawn to one common centre; *and it was solved by Mohammad*" (emphasis ours).

He changed their modes of thought, their customs and their morals. He turned the uncouth into the cultured, the barbarous into the civilised, the evil-doers and bad characters into pious God-fearing and righteous persons. Their unruly and obstinate natures were transformed into models of obedience and submission to law and order. A nation which had not produced a single great man worth the name for centuries gave birth, under his influence and guidance, to thousands of noble souls who went forth to far-off corners of the world to preach and teach the principles of religion, morals and civilisation.[7]

He accomplished this feat not through any worldly lure, oppression or cruelty, but by his humanity, his moral personality and his teaching. With his noble and gentle behaviour he befriended even his enemies. He captured the hearts of the people with his unbounded sympathy and the milk of human kindness. He ruled justly. He did not deviate from truth and righteousness. He did not oppress even his deadly enemies who were after his life, who had stoned him, who had turned him out of his native place, who had set the whole of Arabia against him — nay, not even those who had chewed the raw liver of his dead uncle in a frenzy of vengeance.[8] He forgave them all when he triumphed over them. He never took revenge on anyone.

Although he became the ruler of his country, he was so selfless and modest that he remained very simple and sparing in his habits. He lived poorly, as before, in his humble mud-cottage. He slept on a mattress, wore coarse clothes, ate either the simplest food of the poor or went without food at all. He used to spend whole nights standing in prayer before his Lord. He came to the rescue of the destitute and the penniless.[9] He felt not the least insult in

---

7. It would be instructive to refer here to an important speech of Ja'far ibn Abī Ṭālib. When the oppression of the Muslims of Makka reached its height, the Prophet Muḥammad (blessings of Allah and peace be upon him) asked some of them to migrate to the adjoining state of Abyssinia. A group did so. But the Quraish who were perpetrating every conceivable oppression against the Muslims did not sit by idly. They pursued the Muslims and asked King Negus of Abyssinia to forcefully return his immigrants. In the court of King Negus, Ja'far made a speech which threw light on the revolution that the Holy Prophet had brought about. He said: "O King! We were ignorant people, given to idolatry. We were used to eating corpses even of dead animals, and to doing all kinds of disgraceful things. We did not carry out our obligations to our relations, and ill-treated our neighbours. The strong among us would thrive at the expense of the weak, till, at last, God raised a Prophet for our reformation. His descent, his righteousness, his integrity and his piety are well known to us all. He called us to the worship of God and exhorted us to give up idolatry and stone-worship. He enjoined us to speak the truth, to make good our trusts, to respect ties of kinship, and to do good to our neighbours. He taught us to shun everything foul and to avoid bloodshed. He forbade all manner of indecent things: telling lies, misappropriating orphans' belongings, and bringing false accusation against the chastity of women. So we believed in him, followed him, and acted upon his teaching . . ."

8. On the occasion of the Battle of Uḥud, Hinda, the wife of the chief of the pagan Arabs, actually chewed the raw liver of the Prophet's uncle, Hamza.

9. The Prophet said: "Anyone who dies in debt or leaves behind dependents who are in danger of becoming destitute should come to me because I am their guardian." His whole life bears ample testimony to this.

51

working like a labourer. Till his last moments there was not the slightest tinge of royal pomp or hauteur of the high and mighty in him. Like any ordinary man he would sit and talk with people and share their joys and sorrows. He would so mingle with the crowd that a stranger would find it difficult to single out the leader of the people and the ruler of the nation from the rest of the company.

He never sought any reward or profit for himself, nor left any property to his heirs. He dedicated his all to his *Millah*. He did not ask his adherents to earmark anything for him or his descendants, so much so that he forbade his progeny to receive the benefit of poor-tax *(Zakāh)*.

His Contribution to Human Thought

The achievements of this great man do not end here. To arrive at a full appreciation of his worth one has to view them against the background of the history of the world as a whole. This reveals that this unlettered dweller of the desert of Arabia, who was born in the 'dark ages' some 1400 years ago, is the real pioneer of our modern age. He is not only the leader of those who accept his leadership but also of those who do not, even of those who denounce him — the only difference being that the latter are unaware that he is still imperceptibly influencing their thoughts and their actions and is the governing principle of their lives and the guiding spirit of the modern times.[10]

---

10. Arthur Leonard says: "Islam, in fact, has done a work. She has left a mark on the pages of human history, which is so indelible that it can never be effaced . . . that only when the world grows will be acknowledged in full."
John Devenport, a leading scientist, observed: "It must be owned that all the knowledge, whether of physics, astronomy, philosophy or mathematics, which flourished in Europe from the 10th century, was originally derived from the Arabian schools, and the Spanish Saracen may be looked upon as the father of European philosophy." — Quoted by A. Karim in *Islam's Contribution to Science and Civilisation.*
Bertrand Russell, the famous British philosopher, wrote: "The supremacy of the East was not only military. Science, philosophy, poetry and the arts all flourished . . . in the Muhammedan world at a time when Europe was sunk in barbarism. Europeans, with unpardonable insularity, call this period 'The Dark Ages': but it was only in Europe that it was dark — indeed only in Christian Europe, *for Spain, which was Muhammedan, had a brilliant culture."* — *Pakistan Quarterly,* Vol. IV, No. 3, (emphasis ours).
Robert Briffault, the renowned historian, acknowledges in his book *The Making of Humanity:* "It is highly probably that but for the Arabs, modern European civilisation would never have assumed that character which has enabled it to transcend all previous phases of evolution. *For although there is not a single aspect of human growth in which the decisive influence of Islamic culture is not traceable, nowhere is it so clear and momentous as in the genesis of that power which constitutes the paramount distinctive force of the modern world and the supreme source of its victory* — *natural sciences and the scientific spirit* . . . What we call science arose in Europe as a result of a new spirit of inquiry: of new methods of investigation, of the method of experiment, observation, measurement, of the development of mathematics in a form unknown to the Greeks. That spirit and those methods were introduced into the European world by the Arabs."
Stanwood Cobb, founder of the Progressive Education Association, says: "Islam . . . was the virtual creator of the Renaissance in Europe." — Quoted by Robert L. Gullick, Jr., in *Muḥammad the Educator.*

It was he who turned the course of human thought from superstition-mongering, love for the unnatural and the inexplicable, and monasticism towards a rational approach, love for reality, and a pious, balanced worldly life. It was he who in a world which regarded only supernatural happenings as miracles and demanded them for the verification of the truth of a religious mission, urged that rational proof should be the criterion of truth. It was he who opened the eyes of those who had been accustomed to look for the signs of God in natural phenomena.

It was he who, in place of groundless speculation, led human beings to the path of rational understanding and sound reasoning on the basis of observation, experiment and research. It was he who clearly defined the limits and functions of sense perception, reason and intuition. It was he who brought about a *rapprochement* between spiritual and material values. It was he who harmonised Faith and Knowledge and Action, who, in short, evolved true religiosity on the basis of the scientific spirit.

It was he who eradicated idolatry, man-worship and polytheism in all forms so thoroughly and created such a firm faith in the Unity of God that even those religions which were based entirely on superstition and idolatry were forced to adopt a monotheistic approach.

It was he who changed the basic concepts of ethics and spirituality. Those who believed that asceticism and self-annihilation alone led to moral and spiritual purity — that purity could only be achieved by running away from life, desregarding all the desires of the flesh and subjecting the body to all types of tortures — he showed the path of spiritual evolution, moral emancipation and attainment of salvation through active participation in the affairs of the world around them.

It was he who brought home to man his true worth; those who acknowledged only a God-incarnate or a son of God as their moral preceptor or spiritual guide were told that human beings with no pretensions to Godhead could become vicegerents of God on earth; those who proclaimed and worshipped powerful personages as their gods were made to understand that their false lords were mere ordinary human beings and nothing more. It was he who stressed the point that no person could claim holiness, authority and overlordship as his birthright and that no-one was born with the stigma of untouchability, slavery or serfdom. It was he and his teaching which inspired thoughts of the unity of mankind, equality of human beings, true democracy and real freedom.

Laws which he gave have penetrated deep into the structures of society, and this process continues up to this day. The basic principles of economics which he taught have ushered in many a movement in world history and hold out the same promise for the future. The laws of governance which he formulated brought about many upheavals in political theories and continues to have influence even today. The fundamental principles of law and justice which bear the stamp of his genius have influenced to a remarkable degree the administration of justice in the courts of nations. This unlettered Arab was the first person to formulate a framework of international relations and lay down laws of war and peace. No one previously had even the remotest idea that there could be an ethical code of war and that relations between different nations could be regulated on the basis of common humanity.[11]

The Greatest Revolutionary
In the cavalcade of world history the sublime figure of this wonderful person towers so high above all others that they appear to be dwarfs when contrasted with him. None of them possessed a genius capable of making a deep impression on more than one or two aspects of human life. Some are brilliant theoreticians but are lacking when it comes to practical action. Some are men of action but with little knowledge. Some are renowned as statesmen only, others are masters of strategy. Others again have devoted their energies to ethical and spiritual problems but have ignored economics and politics. In short, one comes across heroes who are expert in one walk of life only.

His is the only example where all the excellences have been blended into one personality. He is a philosopher and a seer as well as a living embodiment of his own teachings. He is a great statesman as well as a military genius. He is a legislator and also a teacher of morals. He is a spiritual luminary as well as a religious guide. His vision penetrates every aspect of life. His orders and commandments cover a vast field from the regulation of international relations down to the habits of everyday life like eating, drinking and personal hygiene. On the foundations of his philosophy he established a civilisation and a culture without the slightest trace of a flaw, deficiency or incompleteness. Can anyone point to another example of such a perfect and all-round personality?

Most of the famous personalities of the world are said to be the products of their environment. But his case is unique. His environment seems to have played no part in the making of his personality. At most one might accept in the light of Hegel's philosophy of history or Marx's historical materialism

---

11. For details, see Abul A'lā Mawdūdī's *Al-Jihād fi'l-Islām*.

54

that the time and environment demanded the emergence of a leader who could create a nation and build an empire. But Hegelian or Marxist philosophy cannot explain how such an environment could produce a man whose mission was to teach the highest morals, to purify humanity and to wipe out prejudice and superstition, who looked beyond the artificial compartments of race and nation-state, who laid the foundations of a moral, spiritual, cultural and political superstructure for the good of the whole world, who practically, not theoretically, placed business transactions, civics, politics and international relations on moral grounds and produced such a balanced synthesis between worldly life and spiritual advancement that even to this day it is considered a masterpiece of wisdom and foresight. Can anyone honestly call such a person a product of the all-pervading darkness of Arabia?

He does not only appear to be independent of his environment. When we look at his achievements we are irresistibly drawn to the conclusion that he actually transcends the limitations of time and space. His vision breaks through all temporal and physical barriers, passes beyond centuries and millenniums and encompasses within itself the whole of human history.

He is not one of those whom history has cast into oblivion, and he is not praised only because he was a good leader in his own time. He is that unique and incomparable leader of humanity who marches with time, who is modern in every age and in every era.

Those whom people style 'makers of history' are only 'creatures of history'. In fact, in the whole of the history of mankind, he is the unique example of a 'maker of history'. One may scan the lives and circumstances of the great leaders of the world who brought about revolutions and one will find that on such occasions the forces of revolution were gathering momentum for the destined upheaval, were taking their course in certain directions and were only waiting for the right moment. In harnessing these forces the revolutionary leader played the part of an actor for whom the stage and the role is set beforehand. On the other hand, the Prophet is the only person who had to genuinely create a revolution; he had to mould and produce the kind of men he wanted because the spirit of revolution and its necessary conditions were non-existent.

He made an indelible impression on the hearts of thousands of his disciples by his forceful personality and moulded them to his way of thinking. By his iron will be prepared the ground for revolution and directed events into the channels he wanted. Can anyone cite another example of a maker of history of such distinction, another revolutionary of such brilliance and splendour?

The Final Testimony

One may wonder how, in the dark ages 1400 years ago in a benighted region of the earth like Arabia, an illiterate Arab trader and herdsman came to possess such light, such knowledge, such power, such capabilities and such finely developed moral virtues?

One may say that there is nothing peculiar about his Message, that it is the product of his own mind. If this is so, then he should have proclaimed himself God. And if he had done so at that time, the peoples of the earth who did not hesitate in calling Krishna and Buddha gods and Jesus the Son of God, and who could without compunction worship such forces of nature as fire, water and air — would have readily acknowledged him as such.

But he argued just the opposite. For he proclaimed: I am a human being like yourselves. I have not brought anything to you of my own accord. It has all been revealed to me by God. Whatever I possess belongs to Him. This message, the like of which the whole of humanity is unable to produce, is the message of God. It is not the product of my own mind. Every word of it has been sent down by Him and all glory to Him Whose Message it is. All the wonderful achievements which stand to my credit in your eyes, all the laws which I have given, all the principles which I have enunciated and taught — none of them is from me. I find myself incompetent to produce such things out of my sheer personal ability and capabilities. I look to Divine Guidance in all matters. Whatever He wills I do, what He directs I proclaim.

Hearken! What a wonderful and inspiring example of honesty, integrity, truth and honour those sentiments are! Liars and hypocrites often try to take all the credit for the deeds of others, even when they can easily be found out. But this great man does not claim any of these achievements for himself even when no-one could contradict him as there was no way of establishing the source of his inspiration.

What more proof of perfect honesty of purpose, uprightness of character and sublimity of soul can there be! Who else can be more truthful than he who received such unique gifts through a secret channel and still pointed out their source? All these factors lead to the irresistible conclusion that such a man was the true Messenger of God.

Such was our Holy Prophet Muhammad (blessings of Allah and peace be upon him). He was a prodigy of extraordinary merits, a paragon of virtue and goodness, a symbol of truth, a great apostle of God and His Messenger to the entire world. His life and thought, his truthfulness and straightforwardness, his piety and goodness, his character and morals, his ideology and achievements — all stand as unimpeachable proofs of his prophethood. Any human being who studies his life and teachings without bias will testify that he was the true Prophet of God and the Qur'ān — the Book he gave to mankind — the true Book of God. No serious seeker after truth can come to any other conclusion.

It must also be clearly understood that now, through Muḥammad (blessings of Allah and peace be upon him) alone can we know the straight path of Islam. The Qur'ān and the life-example of Muḥammad (blessings of Allah and peace be upon him) are the only reliable sources that are available to mankind to learn God's Will in its totality. Muḥammad (blessings of Allah and peace be upon him) is the Messenger of God for the whole of mankind and the long chain of Prophets has come to an end with him. He was the last of the Prophets and all the instructions which it was God's Will to impart to mankind through direct revelation were sent by Him through Muḥammad (blessings of Allah and peace be upon him) and are enshrined in the Qur'ān and the *Sunnah*. Anyone who seeks to become a sincere Muslim must have faith in God's last Prophet, accept his teachings and follow the way he has pointed out to man. This is the road to success and salvation.

The Finality of Prophethood
This brings us to the question of the finality of the prophethood of Muḥammad (blessings of Allah and peace be upon him).

We have already discussed the nature of prophethood and this discussion makes it clear that the advent of a prophet is not an everyday occurrence. Nor is the presence *in person* of the Prophet essential for every land, people and period. The life and teachings of the Prophet are the beacon to guide a people to the right path, and as long as his teachings and his guidance are alive he is, as it were, himself alive.

The real death of a Prophet consists not in his physical demise but in the ending of the influence of his teachings. The earlier Prophets have died because their followers have adulterated their teachings, distorted their instructions, and besmirched their life-examples by attaching fictitious events to them. Not one of the earlier books — Torah, *Zabūr* (Psalms of David), *Injīl* (Gospel of Jesus), for example—exists today in its original text and even the adherents of these books confess that they do not possess the *original* books. The life-histories of the earlier Prophets have been so mixed up with fiction that an accurate and authentic account of their lives has become impossible. Their lives have become tales and legends and no

57

trustworthy record is available anywhere. It cannot even be said with certainty when and where a certain Prophet was born, how he lived and what code of morality he gave to mankind. Thus, the real death of a Prophet consists in the death of his teachings.

By this criterion no-one can deny that Muḥammad (blessings of Allah and peace be upon him) and his teachings are alive. His teachings stand uncorrupted and are incorruptible. The Qur'ān — the book he gave to mankind — exists in its original text, without a word, syllable or even letter having been changed. The entire account of his life — his sayings, instructions and actions — is preserved with complete accuracy. It is as though it all happened yesterday rather than thirteen centuries ago. The biography of no other human being is so detailed as that of Muḥammad, the Prophet of Islam (blessings of Allah and peace be upon him). In everything affecting our lives we can seek the guidance of Muḥammad (blessings of Allah and peace be upon him) and the example of his life. That is why there is no need of any other Prophet after Muḥammad, the last Prophet (blessings of Allah and peace be upon him).

Furthermore, there are three conditions which necessitate the advent of a new Prophet over and above the need to replace a deceased Prophet. These may be summed up as follows:

1. That the teachings of the earlier Prophets have been distorted or corrupted or they have died and their revival is needed.

2. That the teachings of the Prophet who has passed away were incomplete and it is necessary to amend them, improve on them or add something to them.

3. That the earlier Prophet was raised for a particular nation or territory and a Prophet for another nation, people or country is required.[12]

None of these conditions exist today. The teachings of the last Prophet Muḥammad (blessings of Allah and peace be upon him) are alive, have been fully preserved and made immortal. The guidance he has shown unto mankind is complete and flawless, and is enshrined in the Holy Qur'ān. All the sources of Islam are fully intact and each and every instruction or action of the Holy Prophet can be ascertained without the least shadow of doubt.

---

12. Another may be the situation when a Prophet is raised to help and assist another Prophet, but as the instances of such Prophets are very few — in the Qur'ān only two such instances are given — and as this kind of prophethood seems to be the exception rather than the rule, we have not added this as the fourth condition. — Author.

Secondly, God has completed His revealed guidance through the Prophet Muḥammad (blessings of Allah and peace be upon him) and Islam is a complete religion for mankind. God has said that, "Today I have perfected your Faith — religion — for you, and have completed My bounty upon you," and a thorough study of Islam as a complete way of life proves the truth of these Qur'ānic words. Islam gives guidance for life in this world and in the hereafter and nothing essential for human guidance has been left out. There is no ground for new prophethood on the plea of imperfection.[13]

Lastly, the Message of Muḥammad (blessings of Allah and peace be upon him) was not meant for any particular people, place or period. He was raised as the World Prophet — the messenger of truth for the whole of mankind. The Qur'ān has commanded Muḥammad (blessings of Allah and peace be upon him) to declare: "O mankind, I am God's Messenger to all of you." He has been described as "a blessing for all (the people of) the world" and his approach has been universal and human. That is why after him there remains no need for new prophethood and he has been described by the Qur'ān as *Khātam-an-Nabiyyīn* (the last of the chain of the true Prophets).[14]

---

13. Some people say that the passage of time itself is a sufficient ground for the need of new guidance. and a religion which was revealed some thirteen centuries ago must necessarily grow obsolete and become a thing of the past. The objection is totally unfounded. The reasons may be briefly stated as follows:
(a) Islam's teachings are eternal. because they have been revealed by Allah Who knows all the past. present and future and Who Himself is eternal. It is the human knowledge that is limited. It is the human eye which cannot see into the dim vista of the future. not God Whose knowledge is above all the limitations of time and space.
(b) Islam is based on human nature. and the nature of man has remained the same in all times and epochs. All men are cast in the moulds of the earliest men and fundamental human nature remains unchanged.
(c) In human life there is a beautiful balance between permanence and change. Neither is everything permanent, nor is everything changeable. The fundamental principles. the basic values. do not invite change. It is the outward forms which change with the passage of time and which are changed while keeping in view certain principles which are to be observed. And Islam has catered for the needs of both permanence and change. The Qur'ān and the *Sunnah* propounded the eternal principles of Islam. while through *Ijtihād* they are applied to every age according to its own needs. Islam is the only religion which has established machinery for the perennial evolution of human society in accordance with the fundamental principles and permanent values of life.
(d) Scientifically. the human race is living in the age which was inaugurated by the advent of man on earth and no fundamental evolutionary change has occurred in this phase of existence. Civilisations have arisen and died. cultures have grown and withered. empires have emerged and disintegrated. but the age in the great chain of cosmic evolution remains the same. Therefore the view that guidance given some centuries back automatically becomes obsolete with the passage of time is unfounded and superficial. — *Editor.*

14. The Qur'ān and the *Ḥadīth* are very explicit on this point. The Qur'ān says: "Muḥammad is the Messenger of God and the last of the Prophets" (xxxiii. 40).
The Holy Prophet himself has said: "There will be no prophet after me." On another occasion he said: "My relation to the (long chain of the) Prophets can be understood by the parable of a palace: the palace was most beautifully built. Everything was complete therein except the place for one brick. I have filled in that place and now the castle has been completed" *(vide* Bukhārī and Muslim). — *Editor.*

The only source, therefore, for the knowledge of God and His Way is Muḥammad (blessings of Allah and peace be upon him). We can know of Islam only through his teachings which are so complete and so comprehensive that they can guide men through all ages to come. The world does not need a new prophet; it needs only such people as have full faith in Muḥammad (blessings of Allah and peace be upon him), to become the standard-bearers of his message, propagate it throughout the world, and endeavour to establish the culture which Muḥammad (blessings of Allah and peace be upon him) gave to man. The world needs such men of character as can translate his teachings into practice and establish a society which is governed by Divine Law, whose supremacy Muḥammad (blessings of Allah and peace be upon him) came to establish.

This is the mission of Muḥammad (blessings of Allah and peace be upon him) and on its success hinges the success of Man.

Chapter Four

THE ARTICLES OF FAITH

Our discussion so far can be summarised as follows:

1. Islam consists of submission and obedience to Allah, the Lord of the Universe. Since the only authentic source of knowing Him and His Will and Law is the teachings of the true Prophet, we may define Islam as that religion which stands for complete faith in the teachings of the Prophet and steadfast obedience to his ways of life. Consequently, one who ignores the medium of the Prophet and claims to follow God directly is not a 'Muslim'.

2. In earlier epochs there had been separate Prophets for different nations, and the history of prophethood shows that even in one and the same nation several Prophets appeared one after the other. In that age Islam was the name of that religion which was taught to a nation by its own Prophet or Prophets. Though the nature and substance of Islam was the same in every age and country, the modes of worship, codes of law and other detailed rules and regulations of life varied according to local and particular conditions. It was not, therefore, necessary for any nation to follow another nation's Prophet and its responsibility was confined to following the guidance given by its own Prophet.

3. This period of poly-prophetism came to an end with the advent of Muḥammad (blessings of Allah and peace be upon him). The teachings of Islam were made complete through him; one basic law was formulated for the whole world and he was made a Prophet for all mankind. His prophethood was not meant for any particular nation or country or period; his message was for all peoples and for all ages. The earlier codes were abrogated by the advent of Muḥammad (blessings of Allah and peace be upon him) who gave the world a complete code of life. This means there will be no new Prophets and no new religious code until the Last Day. Muḥammad's (blessings of Allah and peace be upon him) teachings are meant for all the children of Adam, the entire human race.

61

Now Islam consists in following Muḥammad (blessings of Allah and peace be upon him), that is, acknowledging his prophethood, believing in all that he has asked us to believe in, following him in letter and spirit, and submitting to all his commands and injunctions, the most fundamental of which is *Lā ilāha illallāh* "There is no deity but Allah".

This brings us to the question: What has Muḥammad (blessings of Allah and peace be upon him) asked us to believe in? What are the articles of Islamic faith? We shall discuss these articles and see how simple, how true, how lovable and how valuable they are and to what high pinnacle they raise the status of Man in this world and the world to come.

Tawḥīd: Faith in the Unity of God

The most fundamental and the most important teaching of Prophet Muḥammad (blessings of Allah and peace be upon him) is faith in the unity of God. This is expressed in the primary *Kalimah* of Islam as "There is no deity but Allah" *(Lā ilāha illallāh)*. This beautiful phrase is the bedrock of Islam, its foundation and its essence. It is the expression of this belief which differentiates a true Muslim from a *kāfir* (unbeliever), *mushrik* (one who associates others with God in His Divinity) or *dahriyah* (an atheist).

The acceptance or denial of this phrase produces a world of difference between man and man. The believers in it become one single community and those who do not believe in it form an opposing group. For the believers there is unhampered progress and success in this world and in the hereafter, while failure and ignominy are the ultimate lot of those who refuse to believe in it.

But the difference between the believers and the unbelievers does not result from the mere chanting of a few words. Obviously, the mere utterance of a phrase or two is not in itself important. The real difference lies in the conscious acceptance of this doctrine and complete adherence to it in practical life. Mere repetition of the word 'food' cannot dull hunger; mere chanting of a medical prescription cannot heal the disease.

In the same way, if the *Kalimah* is repeated without any understanding, it cannot work the revolution which it is meant to bring about. This can occur only if a person grasps the full meaning of the doctrine and accepts and follows it in letter and spirit. We avoid fire because we know that it burns; we keep away from poison because we know that it can kill. Similarly, if the real meanings of *Tawḥīd* are fully grasped, we avoid, in belief as well as in action, every form of disbelief, atheism and polytheism. This is the natural consequence of belief in the Unity of God.

The Meaning of the *Kalimah*

In Arabic the word *ilāh* means 'one who is worshipped', that is, a being which on account of its greatness and power is considered worthy to be worshipped: to be bowed to in humility and submission. Anything or any being possessing power too great to be comprehended by man is also called *ilāh*. The concept *ilāh* also includes the possession of infinite powers and conveys the sense that others are dependent on *ilāh* and that he is not dependent on anyone else. The word *ilāh* carries, too, a sense of concealment and mystery. The word *Khudā* in Persian, *Deva* in Hindi and *God* in English have similar connotations. Other languages also contain words with a similar meaning.[1]

The word *Allāh*, on the other hand, is the essential personal name of God. *Lā ilāha illallāh* literally means "There is no *ilāh* other than the One Great Being known by the name *Allāh*." It means that in the whole of the universe, there is absolutely no being worthy to be worshipped other than Allah, that it is only to Him that heads should bow in submission and adoration, that He is the only Being possessing all powers, that we are all in need of His favour, and that we are all obliged to seek His help. He is concealed from our senses, and our intellect cannot perceive what He is.

Now we know the meaning of these words, let us look more closely at their real significance.

From the earliest known history of man as well as from the oldest relics of antiquity that we have been able to obtain, it appears that in every age man recognised some deity or deities and worshipped them. Even today every nation, from the most primitive to the most advanced, believes in and worships some deity. Having a deity and worshipping him is ingrained in human nature. There is something within man's soul which forces him to do so.

But the question is: what is that thing and why does man feel impelled to do so? The answer to this question can be discovered if we look at the position of man in this huge universe. Neither man nor his nature is omnipotent. He is neither self-sufficient nor self-existing; nor are his powers limitless. In fact, he is weak, frail, needy and destitute.

He is dependent on a multitude of forces to maintain his existence, but all of them are not essentially and totally within his powers. Sometimes they come

---

1. For instance, in Greek it is *Oeo's*, in Latin *Deus*, in Gothic *Guth*, in German *Gott*. For reference, see *Encyclopaedia Brittannica* (Chicago, 1956) Vol. X, p. 460. — *Editor*.

into his possession in a simple and natural way, and at times he finds himself deprived of them. There are many important and valuable things which he endeavours to get, but sometimes he succeeds in getting them, while sometimes he does not, for it is not completely in his own power to obtain them. There are many things injurious to him; accidents destroy his life's work in a single moment; chance brings his hopes to a sudden end; illness, worries and calamities are always threatening him and marring his way to happiness. He attempts to get rid of them, and meets with both success and failure.

There are many things whose greatness and grandeur overawe him: mountains and rivers, gigantic animals and ferocious beasts. He experiences earthquakes, storms and other natural disasters. He observes clouds over his head and sees them becoming thick and dark, with peals of thunder, flashes of lightning and heavy rain. He sees the sun, the moon and the stars in their constant motions. He reflects how great, powerful and grand these bodies are, and, in contrast to them, how frail and insignificant he himself is!

These vast phenomena, on the one hand, and the consciousness of his own frailty, on the other, impress him with a deep sense of his own weakness, humbleness and helplessness. And it is quite natural that a primitive idea of divinity should coincide with this sense. He thinks of the hands which are wielding these great forces. The sense of their greatness makes him bow in humility. The sense of their powerfulness makes him seek their help. He tries to please them so that they may be beneficial to him, and he fears them and tries to escape their wrath so that he may not be destroyed by them.

In the most primitive stage of ignorance, man thinks that the great objects of nature whose grandeur and glory are visible, and which appear to be injurious or beneficient to him, hold in themselves the real power and authority, and, therefore, are divine. Thus he worships trees, animals, rivers, mountains, fire, rain, air, heavenly bodies and numerous other objects. This is the worst form of ignorance.

When his ignorance dissipates to some extent and some glimmers of light and knowledge appear on his intellectual horizon, he comes to know that these great and powerful objects are in themselves as helpless and dependent, or rather, they are still more dependent and helpless. The biggest and the strongest animal dies like a tiny germ, and loses all his power; great rivers rise and fall and become dry; the highest mountains are blasted and shattered by man himself; the productiveness of the earth is not under the earth's control—water makes it prosperous and lack of water makes it barren. Even water is not independent. It depends on air which brings the clouds. Air, too, is powerless and its usefulness depends on other causes. The moon, the sun, and the stars are also bound by a powerful law outside whose dictates they cannot make the slightest movement.

After these considerations man's mind turns to the possibility of some great mysterious power of divine nature which controls the objects he sees and which may be the repository of all authority. These reflections give rise to belief in mysterious powers behind natural phenomena, with innumerable gods governing various parts and aspects of nature such as air, light and water. Material forms or symbols are constructed to represent them and man begins to worship these forms and symbols. This, too, is a form of ignorance, and reality remains hidden to the human eye even at this stage of man's intellectual and cultural pilgrimage.

As man progresses still further in knowledge and learning, and as he reflects more and more deeply on the fundamental problems of existence, he finds an all-powerful law and all-encompassing control in the universe. What a complete regularity is observed in sunrise and sunset, in winds and rains, in the motions of stars and the changes of seasons! With what a wonderful harmony countless different forces are working jointly. And what a highly effective and supremely wise law it is according to which all the various causes in the universe are made to work together at an appointed time to produce an appointed event! Observing this uniformity, regularity and complete obedience to one great law in all fields of Nature, even a polytheist finds himself obliged to believe that there must be a deity greater than all the others, exercising supreme authority. For, if there were separate, independent deities, the whole machinery of the universe would be upset.

He calls this greatest deity by different names, such as *Allāh, Permeshwar, God, Khudā-i-Khudā'igān*. But as the darkness of ignorance still persists, he continues worshipping minor deities along with the Supreme One. He imagines that the Divine Kingdom of God may not be different from earthly kingdoms. Just as a ruler has many ministers, trusted associates, governors, and other responsible officers, so the minor deities are like so many responsible officers under the Great God Who cannot be approached without winning the favour of the officers under Him. So they must also be worshipped and appealed to for help, and should in no case be offended. They are taken as agents through whom an approach can be made to the Great God.

The more a man increases his knowledge, the greater becomes his dissatisfaction with the multiplicity of deities. So the number of minor deities begins to decrease. More enlightened men bring each one of them under the searchlight of scrutiny and ultimately find that none of these man-made deities has any divine character; they themselves are creatures like man, though rather more helpless. They are thus eliminated one by one until only one God remains.

But the concept of one God still contains some remnants of the elements of ignorance. Some people imagine that He has a body as men have, and is in a particular place. Some believe that God came down to earth in human form; others think that God, after settling the affairs of the universe, retired and is now resting. Some believe that it is necessary to approach God through the media of saints and spirits, and that nothing can be achieved without their intercession. Some imagine God to have a certain form or image, and they believe it necessary to keep that image before them for the purposes of worship.

Such distorted notions of godhead have persisted and lingered, and many of them are prevalent among different people even today.

Tawḥīd is the highest conception of godhead, the knowledge of which God has sent mankind in all ages through His Prophets. It was this knowledge with which, in the beginning, Adam was sent down to earth; it was the same knowledge that was revealed to Noah, Abraham, Moses and Jesus (God's blessings be upon them all). It was this knowledge which Muḥammad (blessings of Allah and peace be upon him) brought to mankind. It is Knowledge, pure and absolute, without the least shade of ignorance. Man became guilty of *shirk*, idol-worship and *kufr* only because he turned away from the teachings of the Prophets and depended on his own faulty reasoning, false perceptions or biased interpretations. *Tawḥīd* dispels all the clouds of ignorance and illuminates the horizon with the light of reality.

Let us see what significant realities the concept of *Tawḥīd* — this little phrase: *lā ilāha illallāh* embraces: what truth it conveys and what beliefs it fosters.

First, we are faced with the question of the universe. We are face to face with a grand, limitless universe. Man's mind cannot discern its beginning or visualise its end. It has been moving along its chartered course from time immemorial and is continuing its journey in the vast vista of the future. Creatures beyond number have appeared in it — and go on appearing every day. It is so bewildering that a thinking mind finds itself wonderstruck. Man is unable to understand and grasp its reality by his unaided vision. He cannot believe that all this has appeared just by chance or accident. The

66

universe is not a fortuitous mass of matter. It is not a jumble of unco-ordinated objects. It is not a conglomeration of chaotic and meaningless things. All this cannot be without a Creator, a Designer, a Controller, a Governor.

But who can create and control this majestic universe? Only He can do so Who is Master of all; Who is Infinite and Eternal; Who is All-Powerful, All-Wise, Omnipotent and Omniscient; Who is All-Knowing and All-Seeing. He must have supreme authority over all that exists in the universe. He must possess limitless powers, must be Lord of the universe and all that it contains, must be free from every flaw and weakness and none may have the power to interfere with His work. Only such a Being can be the Creator, the Controller and the Governor of the universe.

Second, it is essential that all these divine attributes and powers must be vested in One Being: it is impossible for two or more personalities having equal powers and attributes to co-exist. They are bound to collide. Therefore, there must be one and only one Supreme Being having control over all others. You cannot think of two governors for the same province or two supreme commanders of the army! Similarly, the distribution of these powers among different deities, so that, for instance, one of them is all-knowledge, the other all-providence and still another life-giver — and each having an independent domain — is also unthinkable. The universe is an indivisible whole and each one of such deities will be dependent upon others in the execution of his task. Lack of co-ordination is bound to occur. And if this happened, the world would fall to pieces. These attributes are also untransferable. It is not possible that a certain attribute might be present in a certain deity at one time and at another time be found in another deity. A divine being who is incapable of remaining alive himself cannot give life to others. The one who cannot protect his own divine power cannot be suited to govern the vast limitless universe.

The more you reflect on the problem, the firmer must your conviction be that all these divine powers and attributes must exist in one and the same Being alone. Thus, polytheism is a form of ignorance that cannot stand rational scrutiny. It is a practical impossibility. The facts of life and nature do not fit in with it. They automatically bring men to Reality, that is Tawḥīd, the Unity of God.

Now, keeping in mind this concept of God, look closely at this vast universe. Exert yourself to the utmost and say if you find among all the objects that you see, among all the things that you perceive, among all that you can think, feel or imagine — all that your knowledge can comprehend — anyone possessing these attributes. The sun, the moon, the stars, animals, birds or fishes, matter, money, any man or a group of men — does any of them possess these attributes? Most certainly not! For everything in the universe is created, controlled and regulated, is dependent on others, is mortal and transitory; its slightest movements are controlled by an inexorable law from which there can be no deviation. Their helpless condition proves that the attire of divinity cannot fit their body. They do not possess the slightest trace of divinity and have absolutely nothing to do with it. It is a travesty of truth and a folly of the highest magnitude to attribute divine status to them.

This is the meaning of La ilaha, (i.e. there is no god) no human and material object possesses the divine power and authority deserving worship and obedience.

But this is not the end of our quest. We have found that divinity is not vested in any material or human element of the universe, and that none of them possesses even the slightest trace of it. This leads us to the conclusion that there is a Supreme Being, over and above all that our eyes see in the universe, Who possesses Divine attributes, Who is the Will behind all phenomena, the Creator of this grand universe, the Controller of its superb Law, the Governor of its serene rhythm, the Administrator of all its workings: He is Allah, the Lord of the Universe and no one and nothing is associated in His Divinity. This is what illallah (but Allah) means.

This knowledge is superior to all other kinds of knowledge and the greater you exert yourself, the deeper will be your conviction that this is the starting-point of all knowledge. In every field of inquiry — be it that of physics, chemistry, astronomy, geology, biology, zoology, economics, politics, sociology or the humanities, you will find that the deeper you probe, the clearer become the indications of the truth of La ilaha illallah. It is this concept which opens up the doors of inquiry and investigation and illumines the pathways of knowledge with the light of reality. And if you deny or disregard this reality, you will find that at every step you meet disillusionment, for the denial of this primary truth robs everything in the universe of its meaning and significance.

Effects of Tawhīd on Human Life
Now let us study the effects which the belief in La ilaha illallah has on the life of a man and see why he should always make a success of life and why one who denies it becomes a failure in life, both here and in the hereafter.

68

1. A believer in this *Kalimah* can never be narrow in outlook. He believes in a God Who is the Creator of the heavens and the earth, the Master of the East and the West and Sustainer of the entire universe. After this belief he does not regard anything in the world as a stranger to himself. He looks on everything in the universe as belonging to the same Lord he himself belongs to. His sympathy, love and service are not confined to any particular sphere or group. His vision is enlarged, his intellectual horizon widens, and his outlook becomes as liberal and as boundless as is the Kingdom of God. How can this width of vision and breadth of mind be achieved by an atheist, a polytheist or one who believes in a deity supposed to possess limited and defective powers like a man?

2. This belief produces in man the highest degree of self-respect and self-esteem. The believer knows that Allah alone is the Possessor of all power, and that none besides Him can benefit or harm a person, or provide for his needs, or give and take away life or wield authority or influence. This conviction makes him indifferent to, and independent and fearless of, all powers other than those of God. He never bows his head in homage to any of God's creatures, nor does he stretch out his hand before anyone else. He is not overawed by anybody's greatness. This attitude of mind cannot be produced by any other belief. For it is necessary that those who associate other beings with God, or who deny God, should bow in homage to some creatures, regard them able to benefit or harm them, fear them and place their hopes in them.

3. Along with self-respect this belief also generates in man a sense of modesty and humbleness. It makes him unostentatious and unpretending. A believer never becomes proud, haughty or arrogant. The boisterous pride of power, wealth and worth can have no room in his heart, because he knows that whatever he possesses has been given to him by God, and that God can take away just as He can give. In contrast to this, an unbeliever, when he achieves some worldly merit, becomes proud and conceited because he believes that his merit is due to his own worth. In the same way pride and self-conceit are a necessary outcome and concomitant of *shirk* (association of others with God in His divinity), because a *mushrik* believes that he has a particular relation with the deities which does not exist between them and other people.

4. This belief makes man virtuous and upright. He has the conviction that there is no other means of success and salvation for him except purity of soul and righteousness of behaviour. He has perfect faith in God Who is above all need, is related to none and is absolutely just. This

belief creates in him the consciousness that, unless he lives rightly and acts justly, he cannot succeed. No influence or underhand activity can save him from ruin. As against this, the *kāfirs* and the *mushriks* always live on false hopes. Some of them believe that God's son has atoned for their sins; some think that they are God's favourites, and will not be punished; others believe that their saints will intercede with God on their behalf; while others make offerings to their deities and believe that by so bribing the deities they acquire a licence to do whatever they like. Such false beliefs keep them enmeshed in sin and evil deeds; depending on their deities, they do not bother about their souls and living pure and good lives. As to atheists, they do not believe that there is any Being having power over them, to Whom they should be responsible for their good or bad actions; therefore they consider themselves independent to act in whatever way they like. Their own fancies become their gods and they live like slaves of their wishes and desires.

5. The believer never becomes despondent. He has a firm faith in God Who is Master of all the treasures of the earth and the heavens, Whose grace and bounty have no limit and Whose powers are infinite. This faith imparts to his heart extraordinary consolation, fills it with satisfaction and keeps it filled with hope. Although he may meet with rejection from all sides in this world, faith in and dependence on God never leave him, and on their strength he goes on struggling. Such profound confidence can result from no other belief than belief in one God. *Mushriks, kāfirs* and atheists have small hearts; they depend on limited powers; therefore in times of trouble they are soon overwhelmed by despair and, frequently, they commit suicide.[2]

6. This belief produces in man a very strong degree of determination, patient perseverance and trust in God. When he makes up his mind and devotes his resources to fulfilling the Divine Commands in order to

---

2. To have an idea of what a harrowing situation this despair of heart can create, the reader is referred to the thought-provoking study of modern life by Mr. Colin Wilson: *The Outsider* (11th impression, London 1957).

The testimony of Prof. Joad is also very explicit on this point. He writes about the West: "For the first time in history there is coming to maturity a generation of men and women who have no religion, and feel no need for one. They are content to ignore it. *Also they are very unhappy, and the suicide rate is abnormally high.*" (C. E. M. Joad, *The Present and Future of Religion*, quoted by Sir Arnold Lunn, *And Yet So New*, London, 1958, p. 228).

As to the world of Islam, let the views of a non-Muslim historian not in any way sympathetic to Islam, be read with profit: "In this uncompromising monotheism, with its simple, enthusiastic faith in the supreme rule of a transcendent being, lies the chief strength of Islam. Its adherents enjoy a consciousness of contentment and resignation unknown among followers of most creeds." *"Suicide is Rare in Muslim Lands"* (Phillip K. Hitti, *History of the Arabs*, 1951, p. 129).

secure God's pleasure, he is sure that he has the support and backing of the Lord of the universe. This certainty makes him firm and strong like a mountain, and no amount of difficulties, impediments and opposition can make him give up his resolution. *Shirk, kufr* and atheism have no such effect.

7. This declaration inspires bravery in man. There are two things which make a man cowardly: (i) fear of death and love of safety, and (ii) the idea that there is someone else besides God who can take away life and that man, by adopting certain devices, can ward off death. Belief in *Lā ilāha illallāh* purges the mind of both these ideas. The first idea goes out of his mind because he knows that his life and his property and everything else really belong to God, and he becomes ready to sacrifice his all for His pleasure. He gets rid of the second idea because he knows that no weapon, no man or animal has the power of taking away his life; God alone has the power to do so. A time has been ordained for him, and all the forces of the world combined cannot take away anyone's life before that time. It is for this reason that no one is braver than the one who has faith in God. Nothing can daunt him: not even the strongest tempest of adversity and the mightiest of armies. Where can the *mushriks*, the *kāfirs* and the atheists get such great determination, force and power from? They hold life the dearest thing in the world; they believe that death is brought about by the enemy and can be warded off by running away from him!

8. The belief in *Lā ilāha illallāh* creates an attitude of peace and contentment, purges the mind of jealousy, envy and greed and keeps away the temptations of resorting to base and unfair means for achieving success. The believer understands that wealth is in God's hands, and He apportions it out as He likes; that honour, power, reputation and authority — everything — is subjected to His will, and He bestows them as He will; and that man's duty is only to endeavour and to struggle fairly. He knows that success and failure depend on God's grace; if He wills to give, no power in the world can prevent Him from so doing; and if He does not will it, no power can force Him to. On the other hand, the *mushriks*, the *kāfirs* and the atheists consider success and failure as dependent on their own efforts and the help or opposition of earthly powers. Therefore, they always remain slaves to cupidity and envy. They never hesitate to turn to bribery, flattery, conspiracy and other kinds of base and unfair means to achieve their ends. Jealousy and envy of others' success eat them away, and they will stop at nothing to bring about the downfall of a successful rival.

71

9. The most important effect of *Lā ilāha illallāh* is that it makes man obey and observe God's Law. One who has belief in it is sure that God knows everything hidden or open and is nearer to him than his own jugular vein. If he commits a sin in a secluded corner and in the darkness of night, He knows it; He even knows our thoughts and intentions, bad or good. We can hide from everyone, but we cannot hide anything from God; we can evade everyone, but it is impossible to evade God's grip. The firmer a man's belief in this respect, the more observant will he be of God's commands; he will shun what God has forbidden and he will carry out His behests even in solitude and in darkness, because he knows that God's 'police' never leaves him alone, and he dreads the Court whose warrant he can never avoid. It is for this reason that the first and the most important conditions for being a Muslim is to have faith in *Lā ilāha illallāh*. 'Muslim', as you have already been told, means one 'obedient to God' and obedience to God is impossible unless one firmly believes in *Lā ilāha illallāh*.

In the teachings of Muḥammad (blessings of Allah and peace be upon him) faith in One God is the most important and fundamental principle. It is the bedrock of Islam and the mainspring of its power. All other beliefs, commands and laws of Islam stand firm on this foundation. All of them receive strength from this source. Take it away, and there is nothing left of Islam.

Belief in God's Angels
The Prophet Muḥammad (blessings of Allah and peace be upon him) has further instructed us to have faith in the existence of God's angels. This is the second article of Islamic faith and is very important, because it obsolves the concept of *Tawḥīd* from all impurities and frees it from the danger of every conceivable shadow of *shirk* (polytheism).

The polytheists have associated two kind of creatures with God:

(a) Those which have material existence and are perceptible to the human eye, such as the sun, moon, stars, fire, water, animals, great men.

(b) Those who have no material existence and are not perceptible to the human eye: the unseen beings who are believed to be engaged in the administration of the universe; for instance, one controls the air, another imparts light, another brings rains, and so on and so forth.

The alleged deities of the first kind have material existence and are before man's eye. The falsity of their claim has been fully exposed by the Kalimah — Lā ilāha illallāh. This is sufficient to dispose of the idea that they enjoy any share in divinity or deserve any reverence at all. The second kind of things, being immaterial, are hidden from the human eye and are mysterious; the polytheists are more inclined to pin their faith in them. They consider them to be deities, gods and God's children. They make their images and render offerings to them. In order to purify belief in the Unity of God, and to clear it from the admixture of this second kind of unseen creatures, this particular article of faith has been expounded.

Muḥammad (blessings of Allah and peace be upon him) has informed us that these imperceptible spiritual beings, whom people believe to be deities of gods or God's children, are really His angels. They have no share in God's divinity; they cannot deviate from His commands even by the slightest fraction of an inch. God employs them to administer His Kingdom, and they carry out His orders exactly and accurately. They have no authority to do anything of their own accord; they cannot present to God any scheme conceived by themselves, they are not even authorised to intercede with God for any man.

To worship them and to solicit their help is degrading and debasing for man. For, on the very first day of man's creation, God had made them prostrate themselves before Adam, granted to him greater knowledge than they possessed and bestowed on Adam His own vicegerency on this earth in preference to them.[3] What debasement can, therefore, be greater for man than prostrating himself before those who had prostrated themselves before him!

Muḥammad (blessings of Allah and peace be upon him) forbade us to worship angels, and to associate them with God in His divinity. He also informed us that they were the chosen creatures of God, free from sin, from their very nature unable to disobey God, and ever engaged in carrying out His orders. Moreover, he informed us that these angels of God surround us from all sides, are attached to us, and are always in our company. They observe and note all our actions, good or bad. They preserve a complete record of every man's life. After death, when we shall be brought before God, they will present a full report of our life's-work on earth, wherein we shall find everything correctly recorded, not a single movement left out, however insignificant and however carefully concealed it may be.

We have not been informed of the intrinsic nature of the angels. Only some

---

3. See Al-Qur'ān, ii. 34 and vii. 11.

of their virtues or attributes have been mentioned to us, and we have been asked to believe in their existence. We have no other means of knowing their nature, their attributes and their qualities. It would therefore, be sheer folly on our part to attribute any form or quality to them of our own accord. We must believe in them exactly as we have been asked to do. To deny their existence is *kufr* for, first, we have no reason for such a denial, and, second, our denial of them would be tantamount to attributing untruth to Muḥammad (blessings of Allah and peace be upon him). We believe in their existence only because God's true Messenger has informed us of it.

Faith in the Books of God

The third article of faith which Muḥammad (blessings of Allah and peace be upon him) has commanded us to believe is faith in the Books of God; Books which He has sent down to mankind through His Prophets.

God had revealed His Books to His Prophets before Muḥammad (blessings of Allah and peace be upon him) and these books were sent down in the same way as He sent down the Qur'ān to Muḥammad (blessings of Allah and peace be upon him). We have been informed of the names of some of these books: Books of Abraham, the Torah of Moses, *Zabūr* (Psalms) of David, and the *Injīl* (Gospel) of Jesus Christ. We have not been informed of the names of Books which were given to other Prophets. Therefore with regard to other existing religious books, we are not in a position to say with certainty whether they were originally revealed books or not.

But we tacitly believe that whatever Books were sent down by God are all true.

Of the Books we have been told, the Books of Abraham are extinct and not traceable in existing world literature. David's *Zabūr*, the Torah and the *Injīl* exist with the Jews and the Christians, but the Qur'ān informs us that people have changed and added to these books, and God's words have been mixed up with texts of their own making. This corruption and pollution of the Books has been so large and so evident that even the Jews and the Christians themselves admit that they do not possess their original texts, and have only their translations, which have been altered over many centuries and are still being changed. On studying these Books we find many passages and accounts which evidently cannot be from God. God's words and those of man are mixed together in these books, and we have no means of knowing which portions are from God and which from man.

We have been commanded to believe in previously revealed Books only in the

74

sense of admitting that, before the Qur'ān, God had also sent down books through His Prophets, that they were all from one and the same God, the same God Who sent the Qur'ān and that the sending of the Qur'ān as a Divine Book is not a new and strange event, but only confirms, restates and completes those divine instructions which people had mutilated or lost in antiquity.[4]

The Qur'ān is the last of the Divine Books sent down by God and there are some very pertinent differences between it and the previous Books. These differences may briefly be stated as follows:

1. The original texts of most of the former Divine Books were lost altogether, and only their translations exist today. The Qur'ān, on the other hand, exists exactly as it was revealed to the Prophet; not a word — nay, not a syllable of it — has been changed. It is available in its original text and the Word of God has been preserved for all time.

2. In the former Divine Books man mixed his words with God's, but in the Qur'ān we find only the words of God — and in their pristine purity. This is admitted even by the opponents of Islam.

3. In respect of no other sacred Book possessed by different peoples can it be said on the basis of authentic historical evidence that it really belongs to the same Prophet to whom it is attributed. In the case of some of them it is not even known in what age and to which Prophet they were revealed. As for the Qur'ān, the evidence that it was revealed to Muḥammad (blessings of Allah and peace be upon him) is so voluminous, so convincing, so strong and so compelling that even the fiercest critics of Islam cannot cast doubt on it. This evidence is so detailed that even the occasion and place of the revelation of many verses and injunctions of the Qur'ān can be known with certainty.

---

4. Even a cursory study of the first books of the Old Testament and the four Gospels of the New Testament reveals that they are the productions of men and in these writings some parts of the original Psalms of David and the Gospels of Christ have been incorporated. The first five books of the Old Testament do not constitute the original Torah, but parts of the Torah have been mixed up with other narrative written by human beings and the original guidance of the Lord is lost. Similarly, the four Gospels of Christ are not the original Gospels as they came from the Prophet Christ (peace be upon him). They are in fact, the life-histories of Christ compiled by four different persons on the basis of knowledge and hearsay, and certain parts of the original Gospel also fell into them. But the original and the fictitious, the Divine and the human, are so intermingled that the grain cannot be separated from the chaff. The fact is that the original Word of God is preserved neither with the Jews nor with the Christians. The Qur'ān, on the other hand, is fully preserved and not a syllable has been changed or left out of it.

75

4. The former Divine Books were sent down in languages which died long ago. No nation or community now speaks those languages and there are only a few people who claim to understand them. Thus, even if the Books existed today in their original and unadulterated form, it would be virtually impossible in our age to correctly understand and interpret their injunctions and put them into practice in their required form. The language of the Qur'ān, on the other hand, is a living language; millions of people speak it, and millions more know and understand it. It is being taught and learnt in nearly every university of the world; every man can learn it, and he who has not time to learn it can find men everywhere who know this language and can explain to him the meaning of the Qur'ān.

5. Each one of the existing sacred Books found among different nations of the world has been addressed to a particular people. Each one contains a number of commands which seem to have been meant for a particular period of history and which meet the needs of that age only. They are neither needed today, nor can they now be smoothly and properly put into practice. It is evident from this that these Books were particularly meant for that particular people and not for the world. Furthermore, they were not sent to be followed permanently by even the people they were intended for; they were meant to be acted upon only for a certain period. In contrast to this the Qur'ān is addressed to all mankind; not a single injunction of it can be suspected as having been addressed to a particular people. In the same manner, all the commands and injunctions in the Qur'ān can be acted upon at any place and in any age. This proves that the Qur'ān is meant for the whole world, and is an eternal code for human life.

6. There is no denying the fact that the previous divine Books also enshrined good and virtue; they also taught the principles of morality and truthfulness and presented the mode of living which was to God's pleasure. But none of them was comprehensive enough to embrace all that is necessary for a virtuous human life. Some of them excelled in one respect, others in some other. It is the Qur'ān and the Qur'ān alone which enshrined not only all that was good in the former Books but also perfects the way of Allah and presents it in its entirety and outlines that code of life which comprehends all that is necessary for man on this earth.

7. On account of man's interpolations, many things have been inserted in those Books which are against reality, revolting to reason and an affront

to every instinct of justice. There are things which are cruel and unjust, and vitiate man's beliefs and actions. Furthermore, things have unfortunately been inserted that are obscene, indecent and highly immoral. The Qur'ān is free of all such rubbish. It contains nothing against reason, and nothing that can be proved wrong. None of its injunctions is unjust; nothing in it is misleading. Of indecency and immorality not a trace can be found. From the beginning to the end the Book is full of wisdom and truth. It contains the best of philosophy and the choicest of law for human civilisation. It points out the right path and guides man to success and salvation.

It is on account of these special features of the Qur'ān that all the peoples of the world have been directed to have faith in it, to give up all other Books and to follow it alone.

The study of the difference between the Qur'ān and other divine Books makes one easily understand that the nature of faith in the Qur'ān and of belief in the former Books are not similar.

Faith in the earlier divine Books should be limited to the confirmation that they were all from God, were true and were sent down to fulfil, in their time, the same purpose for which the Qur'ān has been sent. On the other hand, belief in the Qur'ān should be of the nature that *it is purely and absolutely God's own words*, that *it is perfectly true*, that *every word of it is preserved*, that *everything mentioned therein is right*, that *it is the bounden duty of man to carry out in his life each and every command of it* and that *whatever be against it must be rejected*.

Faith in God's Prophets
In the last chapter we explained that God's Messengers had been raised among every people, and that they all brought essentially that same religion — Islam — which the Prophet Muḥammad (blessings of Allah and peace be upon him) propagated. In this respect all the Messengers of God stand on a par with each other. If a man belies any one of them, he, as it were, belies all, and if a man affirms and believes in one of them, he must and ought to affirm all. The reason is simple. Suppose ten men make one and the same statement; if you admit one of them to be true, you *ipso facto* admit the remaining nine as true, and if you belie any one of them, by implication you belie all of them. It is for this reason that in Islam it is necessary to have implicit faith in all the Prophets of God. One who does not believe in a particular Prophet would be a *Kāfir*, though he may profess faith in all the other Prophets.

Tradition has it that the total number of Prophets sent to different peoples at different times is 124,000. If you consider the life of the world since it was first inhabited and the number of different peoples and nations that have been on it, this number will not appear too great. We have to positively believe in those of the Prophets whose names have been mentioned in the Qur'ān. Regarding the rest, we are instructed to believe that all the Prophets sent by God for the guidance of mankind were true.

Thus we believe in all the Prophets raised in India, China, Persia, Egypt, Africa, Europe and other countries of the world, but we are not in a position to be definite about a particular person outside the list of Prophets named in the Qur'ān, whether or not he was a Prophet, for we have not been told anything definite about him. Nor are we permitted to say anything against the holy men of other religions. It is quite possible that some of them might have been God's Prophets, and their followers corrupted their teachings after their demise, just as the followers of Moses and Jesus (peace be upon them) have done. Therefore, whenever we express any opinion about them, it should be about the tenets and rituals of their religions; as for the founders of those religions, we will remain scrupulously silent, lest we should become guilty of irreverence towards a Prophet.

All the Prophets of God have been deputed by Him to teach the same straight path of 'Islam'. In this sense there is no difference between Muḥammad and other Prophets (blessings of Allah and peace be upon them all), and we have been ordered to believe in all of them alike. But in spite of this equality, there are the following three differences between them:

1. The Prophets of the past came to certain people for certain periods of time, while Muḥammad (blessings of Allah and peace be upon him) has been sent for the whole world and for all time to come.[5]

2. The teachings of those Prophets have either disappeared altogether from the world, or whatever of them remains is intermingled with many erroneous and fictitious statements. For this reason, even if anyone wishes to follow their teachings, he cannot do so. In contrast to this, the teachings of Muḥammad (blessings of Allah and peace be upon him), his biography, his discourses, his way of living, his morals, habits and virtues, in short, all the details of his life and work, are preserved. Muḥammad (blessings of Allah and peace be upon him), therefore, is the only one of the whole line of Prophets who is a living personality, and in whose footsteps it is possible to follow correctly and confidently.

5. This point has been discussed in detail in Chapter Three.

3. The guidance imparted through the Prophets of the past was not complete. Every Prophet was followed by another who effected alterations and additions in the teachings and injunctions of his predecessors and, in this way, the chain of reform and progress continued. That is why the teachings of the earlier Prophets, after the lapse of time, were lost in oblivion. Obviously there was no need to preserve earlier teachings when amended and improved guidance had taken their place. At last the most perfect code of guidance was imparted to mankind through Muḥammad (blessings of Allah and peace be upon him) and all previous codes were automatically abrogated, for it is futile and imprudent to follow an incomplete code when the complete code exists. He who follows Muḥammad (blessings of Allah and peace be upon him) follows all the Prophets, for whatever was good and eternally workable in their teachings has been embodied in his teachings. Whoever, therefore, rejects and refuses to follow Muḥammad's (blessings of Allah and peace be upon him) teachings, and chooses to follow some other Prophet, only deprives himself of that vast amount of useful and valuable instruction and guidance which is embodied in Muḥammad's (blessings of Allah and peace be upon him) teachings, which never existed in the books of the earlier Prophets and which was revealed only through the Last of the Prophets.

This is why it is incumbent on each and every human being to have faith in Muḥammad (blessings of Allah and peace be upon him) and follow him alone. To become a true Muslim (a follower of the Prophet's way of life) it is necessary to have complete faith in Muḥammad (blessings of Allah and peace be upon him) and to affirm that:

(a) He is a true Prophet of God;

(b) His teachings are absolutely perfect, free from any defect or error; and

(c) He is the Last Prophet of God. After him no Prophet will appear among any people till the Day of Judgement, nor is any such personage going to appear in whom it would be essential for a Muslim to believe.

Belief in Life After Death

The fifth article of Islamic Faith is belief in life after death. The Prophet Muḥammad (blessings of Allah and peace be upon him) has directed us to believe in resurrection after death and in the Day of Judgement. The essential ingredients of this belief, as taught to us by him, are as follows:

That the life of this world and of all that is in it will come to an end on an appointed day. Everything will be annihilated. That day is called *Qiyāmah*, i.e. the Last Day.

That all the human beings who have lived in the world since its inception will then be restored to life and will be presented before God Who will sit in judgement on that day. This is called *Ḥashr* (Resurrection).

That the entire record of every man and woman — of all their doings and misdoings — will be presented before God for final judgement.

That one who excels in goodness will be rewarded; one whose evils and wrongs outweigh his good deeds will be punished.

That those who emerge successful in this judgement will go to Paradise and the doors of eternal bliss will be opened to them; those who are condemned and deserve punishment will be sent to Hell — the abode of fire and torture.

The Need of this Belief
Belief in life after death has always been an integral part of the teachings of the Prophets. Every Prophet asked his followers to believe in it, in the same way as the last of the Prophets, Muḥammad (blessings of Allah and peace be upon him), has asked us to do. This has always been an essential condition of being a Muslim. All Prophets have categorically declared that one who does not believe in it, or casts doubts on it, is a *Kāfir*. This is so because denial of life after death makes all other beliefs meaningless. This denial also destroys the very sanction for a good life and man is driven to a life of ignorance and disbelief. A little reflection makes this quite clear.

In your everyday life, whenever you are asked to do anything, you immediately think: what is the use of doing it and what harm is involved in not doing it? This is in the very nature of man. He instinctively regards a useless action as totally unnecessary. You will never be willing to waste your time and energy in useless and unproductive jobs. Similarly, you will not be very eager to avoid a thing that is harmless. And the general rule is that the deeper your conviction about the utility of a thing, the firmer will be your response to it; and the more doubtful you are about its efficacy, the more wavering will be your attitude. After all, why does a child put his hand into fire? Because he is not sure that fire burns. Why does he evade study? Because he does not fully grasp the importance and benefits of education and does not believe in what his elders try to impress on his mind.

Now think of the man who does not believe in the Day of Judgement. Will he not consider belief in God and a life in accordance with His code of no consequence? What value will he attach to a life in pursuit of His pleasure? To him neither obedience to God is of any advantage, nor disobedience to Him of any harm. How, then, can it be possible for him to scrupulously follow the injunctions of God, His Prophet, and His Book? What incentive will there be for him to undergo trials and sacrifices and to avoid worldly pleasures? And if a man does not follow the code of God and lives according to his own likes and dislikes, of what use is his belief in the existence of God, if indeed he has any such belief?

That is not all. If you reflect still deeper, you will come to the conclusion that belief in life after death is the most decisive factor in the life of a man. Its acceptance or rejection determines the very course of his life and behaviour.

A man who has in view success or failure in this world alone will be concerned with immediate benefits and ills. He will not be prepared to undertake any good act if he has no hope of gaining thereby some worldly interest, nor will he be keen to avoid any wrong act if it is not injurious to his interests in this world.

But a man who believes in the next world as well and is convinced of the final consequences of his acts will look on all worldly gains and losses as temporary and transitory and will not put his eternal bliss at stake for a passing gain. He will look on things in their wider perspective and always keep the permanent benefit or harm in view. He will do the good, however costly it may be to him in terms of worldly gains, or however injurious it may be to his immediate interests; and he will avoid the wrong, however tempting it may look. He will judge things from the viewpoint of their eternal consequences and not according to his whims and caprices.

Thus there is a radical difference between the beliefs, approaches and lives of the two persons. One's idea of a good act is limited to whether in this brief temporary life it will bring gain in the shape of money, property, public applause and similar other things which give him position, power, reputation and worldly happiness. Such things become his objectives in life. Fulfilment of his own wishes and self-aggrandizement become the be-all and end-all of his life. And he does not draw back even from cruel and unjust means to achieve his ends. Similarly, his conception of a wrong act is one which may involve a risk or injury to his interests in this world such as loss of property and life, harming of health, blackening of reputation or some other unpleasant consequence.

In contrast to this man, the believer's concept of good and evil will be quite different. To him all that pleases God is good and all that invokes His displeasure and wrath is evil. A good act, according to him, will remain good even if it brings no benefit to him in this world, or even entails loss of some worldly possession or injury to his personal interests. He will be confident that God will reward him in the eternal life and will be the real success. Similarly, he will not fall prey to evil deeds merely for some worldly gain, for he knows that even if he escapes punishment in his short worldly life, in the end he will be the loser because he will not be able to escape punishment from the court of God. He does not believe in the relativity of morals but sticks to the absolute standards revealed by God and lives according to them irrespective of gain or injury in this world.

Thus it is the belief or disbelief in life after death which makes man adopt different courses in life. For one who does not believe in the Day of Judgement it is absolutely impossible to fashion his life as suggested by Islam.

Islam says "In the way of God give charity (zakāh) to the poor." His answer is: "No, zakāh will lessen my wealth; I will, instead, take interest on my money." And in its collection he will not hesitate to take everything belonging to the debtors however poor or hungry they may be. Islam says: "Always speak the truth and shun lying, though you may gain ever so much by lying and lose ever so much by speaking the truth." But his reply will be "Well, what shall I do with a truth which is of no use to me here, and which instead brings loss to me; and why should I avoid lying where it can bring benefit to me without any risk, even that of a bad name?" He visits a lonely place and finds a precious metal lying there; in such a situation Islam says: "This is not your property, do not take it," but he would say: "This is a thing I have come by without any cost or trouble; why should I not have it? There is no one to see me pick this up, no one who might report it to the police or give evidence against me in a court of law, or give me a bad name among the people. Why should I not make use of this valuable?" Someone secretly keeps a deposit with this man, and eventually he dies. Islam says: "Be honest with the property deposited with you and give it over to the heirs of the deceased." He says: "Why? There is no evidence of his property being with me; his children also have no knowledge of it. When I can appropriate it without any difficulty, without any fear of legal claim, or stain on my reputation, why should I not do so?"

In short, at every step in life, Islam will direct him to walk in a certain direction and adopt a certain attitude and course of behaviour; but he will go in the opposite direction. For Islam measures and values everything from the viewpoint of its eternal consequence; while such a person always has in view only the immediate and earthly outcome. Now, you can understand why a man cannot be a Muslim without belief in the Day of Judgement. To be a Muslim is a very great thing; the fact is that one cannot even become a good man without this belief, for the denial of the Day of Judgement degrades man from humanity to a place even lower than that of the lowest of animals.

Life After Death: A Rational Vindication
So far we have discussed the need and importance of belief in the Day of Judgement. Now let us consider how far the constituents of the belief are rationally understandable. The fact is that whatever Muḥammad (blessings of Allah and peace be upon him) has told us about life after death is clearly borne out by reason. Although our belief in that Day is based on our implicit trust in the Messenger of God, rational reflection not only confirms this belief but also reveals that Muḥammad's (blessings of Allah and peace be upon him) teachings in this respect are much more reasonable and understandable than any other viewpoint about life after death.

The following viewpoints are found about life after death:

1. Some people say that there is nothing left of man after death, and that after this life-ending event there is no other life. According to these people, belief in life after death has no reality. They say it is scientifically impossible. This is the view of the atheists who also claim to be scientific in their approach and bring in Western science to support their arguments.

2. Other people maintain that man, in order to bear the consequences of his deeds, is repeatedly regenerated in this world. If he lives a bad life, he will assume in the next generation the shape of some animal, such as a dog or a cat, or some tree or some lower kind of man. If his acts have been good, he will be reborn as a man into a higher class. This viewpoint is found in some Eastern religions.

3. There is a third viewpoint which calls for belief in the Day of Judgement, the Resurrection, man's presence in the Divine Court, and the meting out of reward and punishment. This is the common belief of all the Prophets.

Now let us consider these viewpoints one by one.

The first group, which arrogates to itself the authority and support of science, alleges that there is no life after death. They say that they have never seen anybody coming back from the dead. After death a man is reduced to dust; therefore, death is the end of life and there is no life after death. But consider this reasoning: is this really a scientific argument? Is the claim really founded on reason? If they have not seen a single case of revival after death, they can only say that *they do not know what will happen after death*. But, instead of remaining within this limit, they declare that *nothing will happen after death,* at the same time alleging that they speak out of knowledge! In fact they merely generalise on ignorance. Science tells us nothing — negative or positive — in this respect and their assertion that life after death has no existence is totally unfounded. Their claim is not dissimilar to the claim of an ignoramus who has not seen an aeroplane and on that 'knowledge' proclaims that aeroplanes do not exist at all! Because somebody has not seen a thing, it does not mean that that thing does not exist. No man, not even the whole of humanity, if it has not seen a thing, can claim that such a thing does not, or cannot, exist. This claim is out and out unscientific. No reasonable man can give it any weight.

Now look at the beliefs of the second group. According to them, a human being is a human being because in his previous animal form he had done good deeds; and an animal is an animal because previously as a human being he had behaved badly. In other words, to be a man or an animal is the consequence of one's deeds in one's former form. One may well ask "Which of them existed first, man or animal?" If they say man preceded animal, then they will have to accept that he must have been an animal before that, and was given a human form for its good deeds. If they say it was animal they will have to concede that there must have been before that a man who was transformed into an animal for his bad deeds. This leads to a vicious circle; the advocates of this belief cannot settle on any form for the first creature, for every generation implies a preceding generation so that the succeeding generation may be considered as the consequence of the former. This is simply absurd.

Now consider the third viewpoint. Its first proposition is: that "this world will one day come to an end. God will destroy and annihilate the universe, and in its place will evolve another higher and far superior cosmos."

This statement is undeniably true. No doubt can be cast on it. The more we reflect on the nature of the cosmos, the more clearly it is proved that the existing system is not permanent and everlasting; all the forces working in it are limited in their nature, and will one day be exhausted. That is why the scientists agree that one day the sun will become cold and will give up all its energy, stars will collide with one another and the whole system of the universe will be upset and destroyed. Moreover, if evolution is true in the case of the constituents of this universe, why may it not be true for the whole of it? To think of the universe becoming totally non-existent is more improbable than that it will pass into another evolutionary stage, and another, much-improved order of things will emerge.

The second proposition of this belief is that "man will again be given life". Is it impossible? If so, how did the present life of man become possible? It is evident that God Who created man in this world can do so in the next. Not only is it a possibility, it is also a positive necessity, as will be shown later.

The third proposition is that "the record of all the actions of man in this world is preserved and will be presented on the Day of Resurrection". The proof of the truth of this proposition is provided today by science itself. The sounds which we make produce slight waves in the air and die out. It has been discovered that the sound leaves its impression on its surrounding objects and can be reproduced. Gramophone records are made on this principle. From this it can be understood that the record of every movement of man is being impressed on everything which comes into contact with the waves produced by the movements. This shows that the record of all our deeds is completely preserved and can be reproduced.

The fourth proposition is that "on the Day of Resurrection, God will hold His Court and, with just judgement, reward or punish man for his good and bad deeds". What is unreasonable about this? Reason itself demands that God should hold His court and pronounce judgement. We see men doing good deeds and gaining nothing in this world. We see other men doing bad deeds and not suffering for it. Not only this, we see thousands of cases of good acts bringing trouble on the doer, and of bad deeds resulting in the happiness and gratification of the guilty person. When we notice these events happening every day, our reason and sense of justice demand that a time must come when the man who does good must be rewarded and the one who does evil must be punished. If you have a tin of petrol and a match-box, you can set fire to the house of your opponent, and apparently escape every consequence. Does this mean that such an offence has no consequences at all? Certainly not! It means only that its physical outcome has appeared, and the moral outcome is hidden. Do you really think it reasonable that it should never appear? If you say it should, the question is, where? Certainly not in this world, where only the physical consequences of actions manifest themselves fully, and rational and moral consequences do not become apparent.

Results and consequences of this higher category can appear only if there comes into existence another order of things wherein rational and moral laws reign supreme and occupy the governing position and where the physical laws are made subject to them. That is the next world which, as we have said before, is the next evolutionary stage of the universe. It is evolutionary in the sense that it will be governed by moral rather than by physical laws. The rational consequences of man's actions, which are hidden wholly or partly in this world, will then appear. Man's stature will be determined by his rational and moral worth judged in accordance with his conduct in this life of test and trial. There you will not find a worthy man serving under a fool, or a morally superior man in a position inferior to a wretch, as is the case in this world.

The last proposition of this belief is the existence of Paradise and Hell, which is also not impossible. If God can make the sun, the moon, the stars and the earth, why should He not be able to make Paradise and Hell? When He holds His Court, and pronounces just judgements, rewarding the meritorious and punishing the guilty, there must be a place where the meritorious may enjoy their reward — honour, happiness and gratification of all kinds — and another place where the condemned may feel debasement, pain and misery.

After considering all these questions, no reasonable person can escape the conclusion that belief in life after death is highly acceptable to reason and commonsense, and that there is nothing in it which can be said to be unreasonable or impossible. Moreover, when a true Prophet like Muḥammad (blessings of Allah and peace be upon him) has stated this to be a fact, and it involves nothing but what is good for us, wisdom lies in believing in it implicitly and not in rejecting it without any sound reasons.

The above are the five articles of faith which form the foundation for the superstructure of Islam. Their gist is contained in the short sentence known as *Kalimah-ṭayyibah*. When you declare *Lā ilāha illallāh* (there is no deity but Allah), you give up all false deities, and profess that you are a creature of the One God; and when you add to these words *Muḥammad-ur-Rasūlullāh* (Muḥammad is Allah's Messenger) you confirm and admit the Prophethood of Muḥammad (blessings of Allah and peace be upon him). With the admission of his Prophethood it becomes obligatory that you should believe in the divine nature and attributes of God, in His angels, in His Revealed Books and in life after death, and earnestly follow that method of obeying God and worshipping Him which the Prophet Muḥammad (blessings of Allah and peace be upon him) has asked us to follow. That way lies the road to success and salvation.

Chapter Five

PRAYER AND WORSHIP

The earlier discussion has made it clear that the Prophet Muḥammad (blessings of Allah and peace be upon him) has enjoined us to believe in five articles of faith:

1. Belief in one God Who has absolutely no associate with Him in His divinity;

2. Belief in God's Angels;

3. Belief in God's Books, and in the Holy Qur'ān as His Last Book.

4. Belief in God's Prophets, and in Muḥammad (blessings of Allah and peace be upon him) as His Last and Final Messenger; and

5. Belief in life after death.

These five articles make up the bedrock of Islam. One who believes in them enters the fold of Islam and becomes a member of the Muslim community. But one does not become a complete Muslim by mere vocal profession alone. To become a complete Muslim one has to fully carry out in practice the instructions given by Muḥammad (blessings of Allah and peace be upon him) as ordained by God.

For belief in God makes practical obedience to Him incumbent; and it is obedience to God which constitutes the religion of Islam. By this belief you profess that Allah, the one God, alone is your God, and this means that He is your Creator and you are His creature; that He is your Master and you are His slave; that He is your Ruler and you are His subject. Having acknowledged Him as your Master and Ruler, if you refuse to obey Him you become a self-admitted rebel. Along with faith in God, you believe that the Qur'ān is God's Book. This means that you have admitted all the contents of the Qur'ān to be from God. Thus it becomes your bounden duty to accept and obey whatever is contained in it. Along with that, you have admitted Muḥammad (blessings of Allah and peace be upon him) to be God's Messenger, which means that you have admitted that each and every one of his orders and prohibitions are from God. After this admission, obedience to him becomes your duty. You will therefore be a fully-fledged Muslim only when your practice is consistent with your profession.

87

Now let us see what code of conduct Muḥammad (blessings of Allah and peace be upon him) has taught as ordained by God Almighty. The first and foremost things in this respect are the *'Ibādah — the primary duties which must be observed by each and every person professing to belong to the Muslim community.*

The Spirit of *'Ibādah* or Worship

'Ibādah is an Arabic word derived from *'Abd* (a slave) and it means submission. Allah is your Master and you are His slave and whatever a slave does in obedience to and for the pleasure of his Master is *'Ibādah*. The Islamic concept of *'Ibādah* is very wide. If you free your speech from filth, falsehood, malice and abuse and speak the truth and talk goodly things, and do all this only because God has so ordained, they constitute *'Ibādah*, however secular they may appear. If you obey the law of God in letter and spirit in your commercial and economic affairs and abide by it in your dealings with your parents, relatives, friends and all those who come into contact with you, all these activities of yours are also *'Ibādah*. If you help the poor and the destitute, give food to the hungry and serve the afflicted and do all this not for any personal gain but only to seek the pleasure of God, this is all *'Ibādah*. Even your economic activities — the activities you undertake to earn your living and to feed your dependants — are *'Ibādah* if you remain honest and truthful in them, and observe the law of God.

In short, all your activities are *'Ibādah* if they are in accordance with the law of God and your ultimate objective is to seek the pleasure of God. Thus, whenever you do good or avoid evil for fear of God, in whatever sphere of life and field of activity, you are discharging your Islamic obligations. This is the true significance of *'Ibādah,* that is, total submission to the pleasure of Allah, the moulding into the patterns of Islam one's entire life, leaving out not even the most insignificant part.

To help achieve this aim, a set of formal *'Ibādah* (worships) has been drawn up as a course of training. The more assiduously we follow the training, the better equipped we are to harmonise ideals and practices. The *'Ibādah* are thus the pillars on which the edifice of Islam rests.

Ṣalāh

Ṣalāh is the most fundamental and the most important of these obligations. Ṣalāh are the prescribed daily prayers which consist in repeating and refreshing five times a day the belief in which you repose your faith.

You get up early in the morning, cleanse yourself, and present yourself before your Lord for prayer. The various poses that you assume during your prayers are the very embodiment of the spirit of submission; the various recitals remind you of your commitments to your God. You seek His guidance and ask Him again and again to enable you to avoid His Wrath and follow His Chosen Path. You read out from the Book of the Lord and express witness to the truth of the Prophets and also refresh your belief in the Day of Judgement and enliven in your memory the fact that you have to appear before your Lord and give an account of your entire life.

This is how your day starts. After a few hours the *muezzin* calls you to prayers and you again submit to your God and refresh your covenant with Him. You dissociate yourself from your worldly engagements for a few moments and seek audience before God. This once again brings to the fore of your mind your real role in life. After this rededication you revert to your occupations before presenting yourself to the Lord again a few hours later. This again acts as a reminder to you, and you once more refocus your attention on the stipulations of your Faith. When the sun sets and the darkness of the night begins to shroud you, you once more submit yourself to God in prayers so that you may not forget your duties and obligations in the midst of the approaching shadows of the night. After a few hours you again appear before your Lord for your last prayer of the day. Thus before going to bed you once again refresh your faith and prostrate yourself before your God. And this is how you complete your day. The frequency and timings of the prayers never let you lose sight of the object and mission of life in the maze of worldly activities.

It is easy to understand how daily prayers strengthen the foundations of your faith, prepare you for the observance of a life of virtue and obedience to God, and refresh that belief from which springs courage, sincerity, purposefulness, purity of heart, advancement of the soul and enrichment of morals.

Now see how this is achieved. You perform ablution in the way prescribed by the Holy Prophet (blessings of Allah and peace be upon him). You also say your prayers according to the instructions of the Prophet. Why do you do so? Simply because you believe in the prophethood of Muḥammad (blessings of Allah and peace be upon him) and deem it your bounden duty to follow him ungrudgingly.

Why do you not intentionally misrecite the Qur'ān? Is it not because you regard the Book as the Word of God and deem it a sin to deviate from even a letter? In prayers you recite many things quietly and if you do not recite them or make any deviation from them there is no-one to check you. But you never do so intentionally. Why? Because you believe that God is ever watchful, is listening to all that you recite and is aware of things both open and hidden. What makes you say your prayers at places where there is no one to ask you to offer them or even to see you offering them? Is it not because of your belief that God is always looking at you? What makes you leave some important business and hurry towards the mosque for prayers? What makes you break your sweet sleep in the early hours of the morning, come to the mosque in the heat of noon and leave your evening entertainment for the sake of prayers? Is it anything other than your sense of duty — your realisation that you must fulfil your responsibility to the Lord, come what may? And why are you afraid of any mistake in your prayer? Because your heart is filled with the fear of God and you know that you have to appear before Him on the Day of Judgement and give an account of your entire life.

Now look! Can there be a better course of moral and spiritual training than prayers? It is this training which makes a man a perfect Muslim. It reminds him of his covenant with God, refreshes his faith in Him and keeps the belief in the Day of Judgement alive and ever-present before his mind's eye. It makes him follow the Prophet and trains him in the observance of his duties. This is indeed a strict training for matching one's practice to one's ideals.

Obviously, if a man's consciousness of his duties towards his Creator is so acute that he prizes it above all worldly gains and keeps refreshing it through prayers, he will be honest in all his dealings for, otherwise, he will be inviting the displeasure of God which he has all along striven to avoid. He will abide by the law of God in all aspects of his life in the same way as he follows it in the five prayers every day. This man can be relied on in other fields of activity as well, for if the shadows of sin or deceit approach him, he will try to avoid them. If even after such training, a man disobeys the law of God, it can only be because of some intrinsic depravity of his self.

Then, again, you must say your prayers in congregation and especially so the Friday prayers. This creates among Muslims a bond of love and mutual understanding. It arouses in them a sense of collective unity and fosters among them national fraternity. Prayers are also a symbol of equality, for the poor and the rich, the low and the high, the rulers and the ruled, the educated and the unlettered, the black and the white, all stand in a row and prostrate themselves before their Lord. Prayers also inculcate a strong sense of discipline and obedience to an elected leader. In short, prayers train people in all those virtues which make possible the development of a rich individual and collective life.

These are a few of the myriads of benefits we can derive from our daily prayers.[1] If we refuse to avail ourselves of them we, and only we, are the losers. Shirking the prayers can only mean one of two things. Either we do not recognise prayers as our duty or we recognise them as our duty and still shirk them. In the first case, our claim to faith is a shameless lie, for if we refuse to take orders, we no longer acknowledge God's Authority. In the second case, if we recognise His Authority and still flout His Commands, we are the most unreliable of the creatures that ever trod the earth. For if we can do this to the highest authority in the universe, what guarantee is there that we shall not do the same in our dealings with fellow human beings? And if double dealing dominates a society, terrible discord will be the certain outcome!

Fasting
What prayers seek to do five times a day, fasting in the month of Ramaḍān (the ninth month of the lunar year) does once a year. During this period we eat not a grain of food nor drink a drop of water from dawn to dusk, no matter how delicious the dish or how hungry or thirsty we feel. What is it that makes us voluntarily undergo such rigours? It is nothing but faith in God and the fear of Him and the Day of Judgement. Each and every moment during our fast we suppress our passions and desires and proclaim, by so doing, the supremacy of the Law of God. This consciousness of duty and spirit of patience that incessant fasting for a whole month inculcates in us help us strengthen our faith. Rigour and discipline during this month bring us face to face with the realities of life and help us make our life, during the rest of the year, a life of true subservience to His Will.

From yet another point of view fasting has an immense impact on society, for all the Muslims irrespective of their status must fast during the same month. This emphasises the essential equality of men and thus goes a long way towards creating in them sentiments of love and brotherhood. During Ramaḍān evil conceals itself while good comes to the fore and the whole atmosphere is filled with piety and purity.

This discipline has been imposed on us for our own advantage. Those who do not fulfil this primary duty cannot be relied on to discharge their other duties. But the worst are those who during this holy month do not hesitate to eat or drink in public. They show by their conduct that they care nothing for the commands of Allah in Whom they profess their belief as Creator and Sustainer. Not only this, they also show that they are not loyal members of the Muslim community — rather, they have nothing to do with it. Only the worst can be expected of such hypocrites.

---

1. For a detailed discussion of the nature and significance of ṣalāh, see Maulānā Mawdūdī's book: Islāmī 'Ibāadat Par Taḥqīqī Naẓar (A Treatise on Islamic Worship). — Editor.

Zakāh

The third obligation is *Zakāh*. Every Muslim whose finances are above a certain specified minimum must pay $2\frac{1}{2}$ per cent of his cash balance annually[2] to a deserving fellow-being, a new convert to Islam, a traveller or a person with debts.[3] This is the minimum. The more you pay, the greater the reward that Allah will bestow on you.

The money that we pay as *Zakāh* is not something Allah needs or receives. He is above any want and desire. He, in His benign Mercy, promises us manifold rewards if we help our brethren. But there is one basic condition for being thus rewarded: when we pay in the name of Allah, we shall neither expect nor demand any worldly gains from the beneficiaries nor aim at becoming known as philanthropists.

Zakāh is as basic to Islam as other forms of *'Ibādah: Salāh* (prayer) and *Sawm* (fasting). Its fundamental importance lies in the fact that it fosters in us the quality of sacrifice and rids us of selfishness and plutolatry. Islam accepts within its fold only those who are ready to give away in God's way some of their hard-earned wealth willingly and without any temporal or personal gain. It has nothing to do with misers. A true Muslim will, when the call comes, sacrifice all his belongings in the way of Allah, for *Zakāh* has already trained him to do so.

Muslim society has much to gain from the institution of *Zakāh*. It is the bounden duty of every well-to-do Muslim to help his lowly-placed, poor brethren. His wealth is not to be spent solely for his own comfort and luxury — there are rightful claimants on his wealth, and they are the nation's widows and orphans, the poor and the invalid; those who have the ability but lack the means to get useful employment and those who have the talent but not the money to acquire knowledge and become useful members of the community. He who does not recognise the call on his wealth of such members of his own community is indeed cruel. For there could be no greater cruelty than to fill one's own coffers while others die of hunger or suffer the agonies of unemployment. Islam is a sworn enemy of selfishness, greed and acquisitiveness. Disbelievers, devoid of sentiments of universal love, know only how to preserve wealth and to add to it by lending it out on interest. Islam's teachings are the antithesis of this attitude. Here one shares

---

2. *Zakāh* is not merely on the cash balance. It is also charged on gold, silver, merchandise, cattle and other valuables. The rate of *zakāh* for all these commodities can be found in the books on *Fiqh* and is not given here for the sake of economy of space.

3. It should be noted that the Holy Prophet has forbidden his own kith and kin to take *zakāh*. Though it is obligatory on the Hashimites to pay *zakāh*, they cannot receive it even if they are poor and needy. If anybody wants to help a poor Hashimite, he may give him a gift. He cannot be helped out of *zakāh*.

one's wealth with others and helps them stand on their own feet and become productive members of society.

Ḥajj or Pilgrimage

Ḥajj, or the pilgrimage to Makka, is the fourth basic 'Ibādah.

Makka today stands at the site of a small house that the Prophet Abraham (God's blessings be upon him) built for the worship of Allah. Allah rewarded him by calling it His own House and by making it the centre towards which all must face when saying prayers. He also made it obligatory on those who can afford it to visit this place at least once in a lifetime. This visit is not merely a courtesy call. This pilgrimage has its rites and conditions to be fulfilled which inculcate in us piety and goodness. When we undertake the pilgrimage, we are required to suppress our passions, refrain from bloodshed and be pure in word and deed. God promises rewards for our sincerity and submissiveness.

The pilgrimage is, in a way, the biggest of all 'Ibādah. For unless a man really loves God he would never undertake such a long journey leaving all his near and dear ones behind him. And this pilgrimage is unlike any other journey. Here his thoughts are concentrated on Allah, his very being vibrates with the spirit of intense devotion. When he reaches the holy place, he finds the atmosphere filled with piety and godliness; he visits places which bear witness to the glory of Islam, and all this leaves an indelible impression on his mind, which he carries to his last breath.

Then there are, as in other 'Ibādah, many benefits that Muslims can derive from this pilgrimage. Makka is the centre towards which Muslims must converge once a year, meet and discuss topics of common interest, and in general create and refresh in themselves the faith that all Muslims are equal and deserve the love and sympathy of others, irrespective of their geographical or cultural origin. Thus the pilgrimage unites the Muslims of the world into one international fraternity.

Defence of Islam

Although the defence of Islam is not a fundamental tenet its need and importance have been repeatedly emphasised in the Qur'ān and the Ḥadīth. It is in essence a test of our sincerity and truthfulness as believers in Islam. If we do not defend one whom we call our friend against intrigues or open assaults from his foes, or are guided in our actions towards him solely by selfishness, we are indeed false friends. Similarly, if we profess belief in Islam, we must jealously guard and uphold the prestige of Islam. The sole guide in our conduct must be the interest of Muslims at large and the service of Islam, in the face of which all our personal considerations must take a back seat.

Jihād

Jihād is part of this overall defence of Islam. *Jihād* means to struggle to the utmost of one's capacity. A man who exerts himself physically or mentally or spends his wealth *in the way of Allah* is indeed engaged in *Jihād*. But in the language of the *Sharī'ah* this word is used particularly for a war that is waged solely in the name of Allah against those who practise oppression as enemies of Islam.

This supreme sacrifice of life devolves on all Muslims. If, however, a section of Muslims offer themselves for the *Jihād,* the community as a whole is absolved of its responsibility. But if none comes forward, everybody is guilty. This concession vanishes for the citizens of an Islamic State when it is attacked by a non-Muslim power. In that case everybody must come forward for the *Jihād.* If the country attacked has not enough strength to fight back, then it is the religious duty of the neighbouring Muslim countries to help her; if even they fail, then the Muslims of the whole world must fight the common enemy. In all such cases, *Jihād* is as much a primary duty of the Muslims concerned as are the daily prayers or fasting. One who shirks it is a sinner. His very claim to being a Muslim is doubtful. He is a hypocrite whose *'Ibādah* and prayers are a sham, a worthless, hollow show of devotion.

Chapter Six

DĪN AND SHARĪʿAH

So far we have been dealing with *Dīn* or Faith. We now come to a discussion of the *Sharīʿah* of the Prophet Muḥammad (blessings of Allah and peace be upon him). But let us first be clear about the difference between *Dīn* and *Sharīʿah*.

Distinction Between *Dīn* and *Sharīʿah*

In the foregoing chapters we said that all the Prophets who have appeared from time to time propagated Islam, that is a belief in God with all His attributes, faith in the Day of Judgement and faith in the Prophets and the Books; they asked people to live a life of obedience and submission to their Lord. This is what constitutes *al-Dīn* and it was common to the teachings of all the Prophets.

Apart from this *Dīn* there is the *Sharīʿah*, the detailed code of conduct or the canons comprising ways and modes of worship, standards of morals and life and laws that allow and proscribe, that judge between right and wrong. Such canon law has undergone amendments from time to time and though each Prophet had the same *Dīn*, he brought with him a different *Sharīʿah* to suit the conditions of his own people and time. This process ended with the advent of Muḥammad, the last Prophet (blessings of Allah and peace be upon him), who brought with him the final code which was to apply to all mankind for all times to come. *Dīn* has undergone no change, but all the previous *Sharīʿahs* stand abrogated because of the comprehensive *Sharīʿah* that Muḥammad (blessings of Allah and peace be upon him) brought with him. This is the climax of the great process of training that was started at the dawn of the human era.

The Sources of *Sharīʿah*

We draw upon two major sources to learn about the *Sharīʿah* of Muḥammad (blessings of Allah and peace be upon him), the Qurʾān and the Ḥadīth. The Qurʾān is a divine revelation — each and every word of it is from Allah. The Ḥadīth is a collection of the instructions issued or the memoirs of the last Prophet's conduct and behaviour, as preserved by those who were present in his company or those to whom these were handed down by the first witnesses. These were later sifted and collected by divines

95

and compiled in the form of books among which the collections made by Malik, Bukhāri, Muslim, Tirmidhī, Abū Dāwūd, Nasāī and Ibn Mājah are considered to be the most authentic.

Fiqh

Detailed law derived from the Qur'ān and the *Hadīth* covering the myriads of problems that arise in the course of man's life have been compiled by some of the leading legislators of the past. The Muslims should forever be grateful to those men of learning and vision who devoted their lives to gaining a mastery of the Qur'ān and the *Hadīth*, and who made it easy for every Muslim to fashion his everyday affairs according to the requirements of the *Sharī'ah*. It is due to them alone that Muslims all over the world can follow the *Sharī'ah* easily even though their attainments in religion are never such that they could themselves give a correct and authentic interpretation of the Qur'ān or the *Hadīth*.

Although in the beginning many religious leaders applied themselves to the task, only four major schools of thought remain. They are[1]:

1. *Fiqh Hanafī:* This is the *Fiqh* compiled by Abū Hanīfa Nu'mān bin Thābit with the assistance and co-operation of Abū Yūsuf Muhammad, Zufar and others, all of whom had high religious attainments to their credit. This is known as the Hanafī School of *Fiqh*.

2. *Fiqh Mālikī:* This *Fiqh* was derived by Mālik bin Anas Asbahi.

3. *Fiqh Shāfi'ī:* Founded by Muhammad bin Idrīs al-Shāfi'ī.

4. *Fiqh Hanbalī:* Founded by Ahmad bin Hanbal.

All of these were given their final form within two hundred years of the time of the Prophet. The differences that appear in the four schools are but the natural outcome of the fact that truth is many-sided. When different persons employ themselves in interpreting a given event, they come out with different explanations according to their own lights. What gives these

1. The periods and present position of the respective *Fiqhs* are as follows:
Abū Hanifa Nu'mān bin Thābit was born in 80 A.H. (699 A.D.) and died in 150 A.H. (767 A.D.). There are approximately 340 million followers of this *Fiqh*, mostly concentrated in Turkey, Pakistan, Bharat, Afghanistan, Transjordan, Indo-China, China and Soviet Russia.
Mālik bin Anas Asbahi was born in 93 A.H. (714 A.D.) and died in 179 A.H. (798 A.D.). There are approximately 45 million followers of this *Fiqh*, mainly concentrated in Morocco, Algeria, Tunis, Sudan, Kuwait and Bahrain.
Muhammad bin Idris al-Shāfi'i was born in 150 A.H. (767 A.D.) and died in 240 A.H. (854 A.D.). He has approximately 100 million followers concentrated mainly in Palestine, Lebanon, Egypt, Iraq, Saudi Arabia, Yemen and Indonesia.
Ahmad bin Hanbal was born in 164 A.H. (780 A.D.) and died in 241 A.H. (855 A.D.). There are some 3 million followers of this *Fiqh*, mainly concentrated in Saudi Arabia, Lebanon and Syria.

various schools of thought the authenticity that is associated with them is the unimpeachable integrity of their respective founders and the authenticity of the method they adopted. That is why all Muslims, whatever school they may belong to, regard all the four schools of thought as correct and true. Even so one can normally follow only one of them in one's life (there is the group of *Ahl-d-Ḥadīth* who believe that those who have the required knowledge and learning should directly approach the Qur'ān and the *Ḥadīth* for guidance and those who are not bestowed with such knowledge and faculties should follow whichever school they like in any particular matter.[2])

Taṣawwuf

Fiqh deals with observable conduct, the fulfilling of a duty to the letter. That concerning itself with the spirit of conduct is known as *Taṣawwuf*. For example, when we say our prayers, *Fiqh* will judge us only by the fulfilment of the outward requirements such as ablution, facing towards the Ka'bah and the timing and the number of *Raka'ahs*. *Taṣawwuf* will judge our prayers by our concentration and devotion and by their effect on our morals and manners. An *'Ibādah* devoid of spirit, though correct in procedure, is like a man handsome in appearance but lacking in character and an *'Ibādah* full of spirit but defective in execution is like a man noble in character but deformed in appearance.

The above example makes clear the relation between *Fiqh* and *Taṣawwuf*. But it is to the misfortune of the Muslims that as they sank in knowledge and character with the passage of time, they also succumbed to the misguided philosophies of nations which were then dominant, partook of them and patched Islam with their perverted dogmas.

They polluted the pure spring of Islamic *Taṣawwuf* with absurdities that could not be justified by any stretch of the imagination on the basis of the Qur'ān and the *Ḥadīth*. Gradually a section of Muslims appeared who thought and proclaimed themselves immune to and above the requirements of the *Sharī'ah*. These people are totally ignorant of Islam, for Islam cannot admit of *Taṣawwuf* that takes liberties with the *Sharī'ah*. No *Ṣūfī* has the right to transgress the limits of the *Sharī'ah* or treat lightly primary obligations *(Farā'iḍ)* such as daily prayers, fasting, *Zakāh* and the *Ḥajj*. *Taṣawwuf*, in the true sense, is an intense love of Allah and Muḥammad (blessings of Allah and peace be upon him) and such love requires a strict obedience to their commands as embodied in the Book of God and the *Sunnah* of His Prophet. Anyone who deviates from the divine commands makes a false claim of his love for Allah and His Apostle.

---

2. Another major school of thought is that of the *Shī'ah* who have founded their own *Fiqh*. — *Editor*.

Chapter Seven

THE PRINCIPLES OF THE *SHARĪ'AH*

Our discussion of the fundamentals of Islam will remain incomplete if we do not cast a glance over the law of Islam, study its basic principles, and try to visualise the type of man and society which Islam wants to produce. In this last chapter we propose to undertake a study of the principles of the *Sharī'ah* so that our picture of Islam may become complete and we may be able to appreciate the superiority of the Islamic way of life.

The *Sharī'ah* — Its Nature and Purport

Man has been endowed with countless powers and faculties and Providence has been very bountiful to him in this respect. He possesses intellect and wisdom, will and volition, faculties of sight, speech, taste, touch and hearing, powers of hand and feet, passions of love, fear, anger and so on. These faculties have been bestowed on him because they are indispensable to him. His very life and success depend on the proper use of these powers for the fulfilment of his needs and requirements. These God-given powers are meant for his service and unless they are used in full measure life cannot become worth living.

God has also provided man with all those means and resources to make his natural faculties function and to achieve the fulfilment of his needs. The human body has been so made that it has become man's greatest instrument in his struggle for the fulfilment of his life's goal. Then there is the world in which man lives. His environment and surroundings contain resources of every description: resources which he uses as a means for the achievement of his ends. Nature and all that belongs to it have been harnessed for him and he can make every conceivable use of them. And there are other men of his own kind, so that they may co-operate with each other in the construction of a better and prosperous life.

These powers and resources have been conferred so that they may be used for the good of others. They have been created for your good and are not meant to harm and destroy you. The proper use of these powers is that which makes them beneficial to you; and even if there be some harm, it must not exceed the unavoidable minimum. That alone is the proper

99

utilisation of these powers. Every other use which results in waste or destruction is wrong, unreasonable and unjustified. For instance, if you do something that causes you harm or injury, that would be a mistake, pure and simple. If your actions harm others and make you a nuisance to them, that would be sheer folly and an utter misuse of God-given powers. If you waste resources, spoil them for nothing or destroy them that too is a gross mistake. Such activities are flagrantly unreasonable, for it is human reason which suggests that destruction and injury must be avoided and the path of gain and profit be pursued. And if any harm be countenanced, it must be only in such cases where it is unavoidable and where it is bound to yield a greater benefit. Any deviation from this is self-evidently wrong.

Keeping this basic consideration in view, when we look at human beings, we find that there are two kinds of people: *first*, those who knowingly misuse their powers and resources and through this misuse waste the resources, injure their own vital interests, and cause harm to other people; and, *second*, those who are sincere and earnest but err because of ignorance. Those who intentionally misuse their powers are wicked and evil and deserve to feel the full weight of the law. Those who err because of ignorance, need proper knowledge and guidance so that they see the Right Path and make the best use of their powers and resources. And the code of behaviour — the *Shari'ah* — which God has revealed to man meets this very need.

The *Shari'ah* stipulates the law of God and provides guidance for the regulation of life in the best interests of man. Its objective is to show the *best way* to man and provide him with the ways and means to fulfil his needs in the most successful and most beneficial way. The law of God is out and out for your benefit. There is nothing in it which tends to waste your powers, or to suppress your natural needs and desires, or to kill your moral urges and emotions. It does not plead for asceticism. It does not say: abandon the world, give up all ease and comfort of life, leave your homes and wander about on plains and mountains and in jungles without bread or cloth, putting yourself to inconvenience and self-annihilation. This viewpoint has no relevance to the law of Islam, a law that has been formulated by God Who has created this world for the benefit of mankind.

The *Shari'ah* has been revealed by that very God Who has harnessed everything for man. He would hardly want to ruin His creation. He has not given man any power that is useless or unnecessary, nor has He created anything in the heavens and the earth which may not be of service to man. It is His explicit Will that the universe — this grand workshop with its multifarious activities — should go on functioning smoothly and graciously so that man — the prize of creation — should make the best and most productive use of all his powers and resources, of everything that has been harnessed for him on earth and in the high heavens. He should use them in such a way that he and his fellow human beings may reap handsome prizes from them and should never, intentionally or unintentionally, be of any harm to God's creation. The *Sharī'ah* is meant to guide the steps of man in this respect. It forbids all that is harmful to man, and allows or ordains all that is useful and beneficial to him.

The fundamental principle of the Law is that man has the right, and in some cases the bounden duty, to fulfil all his genuine needs and desires and make every conceivable effort to promote his interests and achieve success and happiness — but (and it is an important 'but') he should do all this in such a way that not only are the interests of other people not jeopardised and no harm is caused to their strivings towards the fulfilment of their rights and duties, but there should be all possible social cohesion, mutual assistance and co-operation among human beings in the achievement of their objectives. In respect of those things in which good and evil, gain and loss are inextricably mixed up, the tenet of this law is to choose a little harm for the sake of greater benefit and sacrifice a little benefit, so avoiding a greater harm. This is the basic approach of the *Sharī'ah*.

Man's knowledge is limited. Every man in every age does not, by himself, know what is good and what is evil, what is beneficial and what is harmful to him. The sources of human knowledge are too limited to provide him with the unalloyed truth. That is why God has spared man the risks of trial and error and revealed to him the Law which is the right and complete code of life for the entire human race.[1]

The merits and the truths of this code are becoming more and more clear to man with the passage of time and of knowledge. Even today some people do

---

1. It would be instructive to refer here to an example. Look at the colour problem. The world has not yet been able to adopt a rational and human approach towards coloured people. Biology, for a time, was used to sanction colour discrimination. In the United States for the last two centuries the courts upheld the differentiation. Thousands of human beings were coerced, gagged and tortured for the 'crime' that their skin was black. Separate laws were administered to the whites and the blacks. They could not even study under the same roof in the same school or college. It was only on May 17, 1954 that the U.S. Supreme Court ruled that colour discrimination in universities was unjust and against the principle of equality of man. After committing heinous blunders for centuries man came to the view that such discriminations are unjust and should be abolished. But even now there are many who have not realised the truth of this assertion and still stand for segregation, for instance, the Government of the Union of South Africa and the Western population of the African continent. Even in the United States a large number of 'civilised' people have not as yet accepted desegregation. This is how the human mind has dealt with this problem. The *Sharī'ah*, on the other hand, declared this discrimination unjust from the very first day. It showed the right path, the noble course and saved man from error and blunder. The

101

not appreciate all the merits of this code, but further progress of knowledge will throw new light on them and bring their superiority into even clearer perspective. The world is willy-nilly drifting towards the Divine Code— many of those people who refused to accept it are now, after centuries of gropings and trials and errors, being obliged to adopt some of the provisions of this law. Those who denied the truth of the revelation and pinned their faith on unguided human reason, after committing blunders and courting bitter experience, are adopting in one way or another the injunctions of *Sharī'ah*. But after what loss! And even then not in their entirety! On the other hand, there are people who repose faith in God's Prophets, accept their word and adopt the *Sharī'ah* with full knowledge and understanding. They may not be aware of all the merits of a certain instruction, but on the whole they accept a code which is the outcome of true knowledge and which saves them from the evils and blunders of ignorance and of trial and error. Such people are on the right path and are bound to succeed.

The *Sharī'ah* — Rights and Obligations

The scheme of life which Islam envisages consists of a set of rights and obligations, and every human being, everyone who accepts this religion, is enjoined to live up to them. Broadly speaking, the law of Islam imposes four kinds of rights and obligations on every man: (i) the rights of God which every man is obliged to fulfil; (ii) his own rights upon his own self; (iii) the rights of other people over him; and (iv) the rights of those powers and resources which God has placed in his service and has empowered him to use for his benefit.

These rights and obligations constitute the corner-stone of Islam and it is the bounden duty of every true Muslim to understand them and obey them carefully. The *Sharī'ah* discusses clearly each and every kind of right and deals with it in detail. It also throws light on the ways and means through which the obligations can be discharged — so that all of them may be

---

Holy Qur'ān says: "We have made all the children of Adam, i.e. all human beings, respectable and dignified." The Qur'ān again declares: "O ye people! surely We have created you of a male and a female and made you tribes and families so that ye may identify each other. *Surely the noblest of you in the sight of Allah is one who is most pious, most mindful of his duty.*" Similarly, the Holy Prophet says: "O people, verily your Lord is one and your Father is one. All of you belong to Adam, and Adam was made of clay. There is no superiority for an Arab over a non-Arab nor for a non-Arab over an Arab; nor for a white-coloured over a black-coloured nor for a black-skinned over a white-skinned, except in piety. Verily the noblest among you is he who is the most pious" (*vide* Oration of the Prophet on the occasion of the Farewell Pilgrimage).

This is the clear truth which the *Sharī'ah* told to man *more than thirteen centuries ago*, but unguided reason has succeeded only in touching the fringe of it after centuries of waste, losses and blunders, after subjecting hundreds of thousands of people to indiscriminate segregation and after degrading men and corrupting human society. The *Sharī'ah* gives the simplest and the shortest approach to reality and its disregard leads to utter waste and failure. — *Editor*

simultaneously implemented and none of them violated or trampled underfoot.

Now we shall briefly discuss these rights and obligations so that an idea of the Islamic way of life and its fundamental values may be formed.

1. The Rights of God

First of all we must study the ground on which Islam bases the relationship of man to his Creator. The primary and foremost right of God is that man should have faith in Him alone. He should acknowledge His authority and associate none with Him. This is epitomised in the *Kalimah: Lā ilāha illallāh* (there is no god but Allah).[2]

The second right of God on us is that man should accept wholeheartedly and follow His guidance *(Hidāyah)* — the code He has revealed for man — and should seek His pleasure with both mind and soul. We fulfil the dictates of this right by placing belief in God's Prophet and by accepting his guidance and leadership.[3]

The third right of God on us is that we should obey Him honestly and unreservedly. We fulfil the needs of this right by following God's Law as contained in the Qur'ān and the *Sunnah*.[4]

The fourth right of God on us is to worship Him. This is rendered by offering prayers and other *'Ibādah* as described earlier.[5]

These rights and obligations precede all other rights and as such they are discharged even at the cost of some sacrifice of other rights and duties. For instance, in offering prayers and keeping fasts man has to sacrifice many of his personal rights. He has to get up early in the morning for his prayers and in so doing sacrifices his sleep and rest. During the day he often puts off important work and gives up his recreation to worship his Creator. In the month of Ramaḍān (the month of fasts) he experiences hunger and inconvenience solely to please his Lord. By paying *zakāh* he loses his wealth and demonstrates that the love of God is above everything else. In the pilgrimage he sacrifices wealth and takes on a difficult journey. And in *Jihād* he sacrifices money, material and all that he has — *even his own life.*

---

2. This point has already been discussed in detail in Chapter Four.
3. This has been discussed in Chapter Three.
4. See Chapter Four.
5. See Chapter Five.

Similarly, in the discharge of these obligations one has to sacrifice some of the ordinary rights of others and thus injure one's own interests at large. A servant has to leave his work to worship his Lord. A businessman has to stop his business to undertake the Pilgrimage to Makka. In *Jihād* a man takes away life and gives it away solely in the cause of Allah. In the same way, in rendering God's rights one has to sacrifice many of those things which man has in his control, like animals, wealth, etc. But God has so formulated the *Sharī'ah* that harmony and equilibrium are established in the different fields of life and the sacrifice of others' rights is reduced to the barest minimum.

This is achieved by the limits prescribed by God. He has allowed us every facility in the fulfilment of the obligation of *Ṣalāh*. If you cannot get water for ablution, or you are sick, you can perform *tayammum* (dry ablution). If you are on a journey, you can cut short the *Ṣalāh*. If you are ill and cannot stand in the prayer, you can offer it while sitting or lying. The recitation of the prayer is so manageable that they can be shortened or lengthened as one may wish; at times of rest and ease we may recite a long chapter of the Qur'ān, at busy times we may recite a few verses only. The instruction is that in the congregational prayers and in those prayers which occur during business hours, the recitation should be short. God is pleased with the optional devotions *(Nawāfil)*, but He disapproves our denying ourselves sleep and rest and the sacrifice of the rights of our children and of the household. Islam wants us to strike a balance between the various activities of life.

It is similar with fasts. In the whole year there is only one month of obligatory fasting. If you are travelling or ill you can omit it and observe it at some other convenient time of the year. Women are exempted from fasting when they are pregnant and during their menstrual or suckling periods. The fast should end at the appointed time and any delay is disapproved of. Permission is given to eat and drink from sunset to dawn. Optional fasts are highly valued and God is pleased at them, but He does not like you to keep fasts continuously and make yourself too weak to do your ordinary business satisfactorily.

Similarly, look at the case of *zakāh*; the minimum rate has been fixed by God and man has been left free to give as much more as he likes in the cause of Allah. If one gives *zakāh*, one fulfils one's duty, but if one spends more in charity, one seeks more and more of God's pleasure. But He does not like us to sacrifice all our belongings in charity or to deny ourselves and our relatives those rights and comforts which they should enjoy. He does not want us to impoverish ourselves. We are commanded to be moderate in charity.

Then look at the pilgrimage. It is obligatory only for those who can afford the journey and who are physically fit to bear its hardships. Then, it is obligatory to perform it only once in one's life, in any convenient year. If there is a war or any other situation which threatens life, it can be postponed. Moreover, parental permission has been made an essential condition, so that aged parents may not suffer in one's absence. All these things clearly show what importance God has Himself given to the rights of others *vis-à-vis* His own rights.

The greatest sacrifice for God is made in *Jihād*, for in it a man sacrifices not only his own life and property in His cause but destroys those of others also. But, as already stated, one of the Islamic principles is that we should suffer a lesser loss to save ourselves from a greater loss. How can the loss of some lives — even if the number runs into thousands — be compared to the calamity that may befall mankind as a result of the victory of evil over good and of aggressive atheism over the religion of God. That would be a far greater loss and calamity, for as a result of it not only would the religion of God be under dire threat, the world would also become the abode of evil and perversion, and life would be disrupted both from within and without.

In order to escape this greater evil God has, therefore, commanded us to sacrifice our lives and property for His pleasure. But at the same time He has forbidden unnecessary bloodshed, injuring the aged, women, children, the sick and the wounded. His order is to fight only against those who rise to fight. He enjoins us not to cause unnecessary destruction even in the enemy's lands, and to deal fairly and honourably with the defeated. We are instructed to observe the agreements made with the enemy and to stop fighting when they do so or when they stop their aggressive and anti-Islamic activities.

Thus Islam allows only for the minimum essential sacrifice of life, property and other people's rights in the discharging of God's rights. It is eager to establish a balance between the different demands of man and adjust different rights and obligations so that life is enriched with the choicest of merits and achievements.

2. The Rights of One's Own Self
Next come man's personal rights, that is, the rights of one's own self.

The fact is that man is more cruel and unjust to himself than to any other being. On the face of it this may seem astonishing: how can a man be unjust to himself, particularly when we find that he loves himself most? How can he be his own enemy? It seems unintelligible. But deeper reflection shows that it contains a large grain of truth.

The greatest weakness of man is that when he feels an overpowering desire, instead of resisting it, he succumbs to it, and in its gratification knowingly causes great harm to himself. There is the man who drinks: he cannot stop his craving for it and does it at the cost of money, health, reputation and everything that he has. Another person is so fond of eating that in his eating excesses he damages his health and endangers his life. Another person becomes a slave to his sexual appetites and ruins himself in over-indulgence. Still another becomes enamoured of spiritual elevations: he suppresses his genuine desires, refuses to satisfy the physical needs, controls his appetite, does away with clothes, leaves his home and retires into mountains and jungles. He believes that the world is not meant for him and abhors it in all its forms and manifestations.

These are a few of the instances of man's tendency to go to extremes. One comes across such instances of maladjustment and disequilibrium in one's everyday life and there is no need to multiply them here.

Islam stands for human welfare and its avowed objective is to establish balance in life. That is why the *Sharī'ah* clearly declares that your own self also has certain rights upon you. A fundamental principle of it is: "there are rights upon you of your own person."

The *Sharī'ah* forbids the use of all those things which are injurious to man's physical, mental or moral existence. It forbids the consumption of blood, intoxicating drugs, flesh of the pig, beasts of prey, poisonous and unclean animals and carcases; for all these have undesirable effects on the physical, moral, intellectual and spiritual life of man. While forbidding these things, Islam enjoins man to use all clean, healthy and useful things and asks him not to deprive his body of clean food, for man's body, too, has a right on him. The law of Islam forbids nudity and orders man to wear decent and dignified dress. It exhorts him to work for a living and strongly disapproves of him remaining idle and jobless. The spirit of the *Sharī'ah* is that man should use for his comfort and welfare the powers God has bestowed on him and the resources that He has spread on the earth and in the heavens.

Islam does not believe in the suppression of sexual desire; it enjoins man to control and regulate it and seek its fulfilment in marriage. It forbids him to resort to self-persecution and total self-denial and permits him, indeed, bids him, to enjoy the rightful comforts and pleasures of life and remain pious and steadfast in the midst of life and its problems.

To seek spiritual elevation, moral purity, nearness to God and salvation in the life to come, it is not necessary to abandon this world. Instead, the trial of man lies in this world and he should remain in its midst and follow the way of Allah in it. The road to success lies in following the Divine Law in the midst of life's complexities, not outside it.

Islam forbids suicide and impresses on man that life belongs to God. It is a trust which God has bestowed for a certain period of time so that you may make the best use of it — it is not meant to be harmed or destroyed in a frivolous way.

This is how Islam instils in the mind of man that his own person, his own self, possesses certain rights and it is his obligation to discharge them as best he can, in the ways that have been suggested by the *Shari'ah*. This is how he can be true to his own self.

3. The Rights of Other Men

On the one hand the *Shari'ah* has enjoined man to fulfil his personal rights and be just to his own self, and on the other, it has asked him to seek their fulfilment in such a way that the rights of other people are not violated. The *Shari'ah* has tried to strike a balance between the rights of man and the rights of society so that no conflict arises and there is co-operation in establishing the law of God.

Islam has strictly forbidden the telling of a lie in any shape or form, for lies sully the liar, harm other people and become a source of menace to society. It has totally forbidden theft, bribery, forgery, cheating, the levying of interest and usury, for whatever man gains by these means is obtained by causing loss and injury to others. Back-biting, tale-telling and slander have been forbidden. Gambling, lottery, speculation and all games of chance have been prohibited, for in all of them one person gains at the expense of thousands of losers.

All those forms of exploitative commerce have been prohibited in which one party alone is to be the loser. Monopoly, hoarding, blackmarketing, holding of land from cultivation and all other forms of individual and social aggrandizement have been prohibited. Murder, bloodspilling and spreading of mischief, disorder and destruction have been made crimes, for no-one has a right to take away the life or property of other people merely for his personal gain or gratification.

Adultery, fornication and unnatural sexual indulgence have been strictly prohibited for they not only vitiate the morality and impair the health of the perpetrator but also spread corruption and immorality in society, cause venereal disease, damage both public health and the morals of the coming generations, upset relations between man and man and split the very fabric of the cultural and social structure of the community. Islam seeks to eliminate, root and branch, such crimes.

All these limitations and restrictions have been imposed by the law of Islam to prevent a man encroaching on the rights of others. Islam does not want a man to become so selfish and self-centred that for the attainment of a few desires of the mind and body he unashamedly assails the rights of others and violates morality. The law of Islam so regulates life that the welfare of one and all may be achieved. But for the attainment of human welfare and cultural advancement, negative restrictions alone are not sufficient. In a peaceful and prosperous society people should not only not violate the rights of others and injure their interests but should positively co-operate with each other and establish mutual relations and social institutions that contribute towards the welfare of all and the establishment of an ideal human society. The *Shari'ah* has guided us in this respect as well. We therefore propose to give here a brief summary of those injunctions of Islamic law which throw light on this aspect of life and society.

Family is the first cradle of man. It is here that the primary character-traits of man are set. As such it is not only the cradle of man but also the cradle of civilisation. Therefore, let us first consider the injunctions of the *Shari'ah* relating to the family.

A family consists of the husband, the wife and their children. The Islamic injunctions about the family are very explicit. They assign to man the responsibility for earning and providing the necessities of life for his wife and children and for protecting them from all the vicissitudes of life. To the woman it assigns the duty of managing the household, training and bringing up children in the best possible way, and providing her husband and children with the greatest possible comfort and contentment. The duty of the children is to respect and obey their parents, and, when they are grown up, to serve them and provide for their needs.

To make the household a well-managed and well-disciplined institution, Islam has adopted the following two measures:

(a) The husband has been given the position of head of the family. No institution can work smoothly unless it has a chief administrator. You cannot think of a school without a headmaster or a city without an administrator. If there is nobody to control an institution, chaos results. If everybody in the family goes his own way, nothing but confusion will prevail. If the husband goes one way and the wife another, the future of the children will be ruined. There must be someone as the head of the family so that discipline may be maintained. Islam gives this position to the husband and in this way makes the family a well-disciplined primary unit of civilisation and a model for society at large.

(b) The head of the family has responsibilities. It is his duty to work, and do all those tasks which are performed outside the household. Woman has been freed from all activities outside the household so that she may devote herself fully to duties in the home and in the rearing of her children — the future guardians of the nation. Women have been ordered to remain in their houses and discharge the responsibilities assigned to them. Islam does not want to tax them doubly: to bring up their children and maintain the household, as well as to earn a living and do outdoor jobs would be a clear injustice. Islam, therefore, effects a functional division of labour between the sexes.[6]

But this does not mean that the woman is not allowed to leave the house at all. She is, when necessary. The law has specified the home as her special field of work and has stressed that she should attend to the improvement of home life. Whenever she has to go out, certain formalities should be observed.

---

6. After tasting the bitter consequences of destroying this functional distribution, even some Western thinkers are talking in terms of women going back to their homes. Here are the views of two leading thinkers:

Dr. Fulton J. Sheen writes in *Communism and the Conscience of the West:* "The disturbance of family life in America is more desperate than at any other period in our history. The family is the barometer of the nation. What the average home is that is America: if the average home is living on credit, spending money lavishly, running into debt, then America will be a nation which will pile national debt on national debt until the day of the Great Collapse. If the average husband and wife are not faithful to their marriage vows, then America will not insist on fidelity to the Islamic Charter and the Four Freedoms. If there is a deliberate frustration of the fruits of love, then the nation will develop economic policies of growing undue cotton, throwing coffee into the sea and frustrating nature for the sake of economic prices. If the husband and wife live only for themselves and not for each other, if they fail to see that their individual happiness is conditional on mutuality, then we shall have a country where capital and labour fight like husband and wife, both making social life barren and economic peace impossible. If the husband or wife permits outside solicitations to woo one away from the other, then we shall become a nation where alien philosophies will infiltrate, as Communism sweeps away that basic loyalty which was known as patriotism. If husband and wife live as if there is no God, then America shall have bureaucrats' pleading for atheism as a national policy repudiating the Declaration of Independence and denying that all our rights and liberties come to us from God. It is the home which decides the nation. What happens in the family will happen later in the Congress, the White House and the Supreme Court. Every country gets the kind of Government it deserves. As we live in the house, so shall the nation live." Professor Cyril Joad goes to the extent of clearly saying that: "I believe the world would be a happier place if women were content to look after their homes and their children, even if some slight lowering of the standards of living were involved thereby." (*Variety,* December 1, 1952.)

It is a general rule that the sphere of the family widens through blood-relations and marriage connections. To bind together the members of the family into a unity, to keep their mutual relations close and healthy, and to make each one of them a source of support, strength and contentment to the other, the law of Islam has formulated certain basic laws and rules which embody the wisdom of the ages. They may be summed up as follows:

1. Marriage between those persons who have naturally and circumstantially the closest association and affiliations with each other have been prohibited. Marriage is forbidden between: mother and son, father and daughter, step-father and step-daughter, step-mother and step-son, brother and sister, foster-brother and foster-sister, paternal uncle and his niece, aunt (father's or mother's sister) and her nephew, maternal uncle and his niece, mother-in-law and her son-in-law, and father-in-law and his daughter-in-law. This prohibition strengthens the bonds of the family and makes relations between these relatives absolutely pure and unalloyed: and they can mix with each other without any restraint and with sincere affection.

2. Beyond the limits of the forbidden marriage relations given above, matrimonial relations can be effected between the members of kindred families, so that such relationship may bind them still closer. Marriage connections between two families which are freely associated with each other, and which therefore know each other's habits, customs and traditions, are generally successful. Therefore the *Shari'ah* has not only permitted them but also encouraged and preferred relations with kindred families to those of entirely strange families (though this is not forbidden).

3. In a group of kindred families, there usually co-exists the rich and the poor, the prosperous and the destitute. The Islamic principle is that a man's relatives have the greatest right on him. Respect for the tie between relatives is technically called *Ṣilah-al-raḥm*. Muslims are enjoined to respect this bond in every possible way. To be disloyal to one's relatives and to be negligent of their rights is a great sin and God has disapproved of it. If a relative becomes poor, or is beset by some trouble, it is the duty of his rich and prosperous relatives to help him. Special regard for the rights of relatives has been enjoined in *Zakāh* and other charities.

4. The law of inheritance is so formulated in Islam that property left by the deceased cannot be concentrated in one place. It is distributed in such

a way that all near relatives get their share. Son, daughter, wife, husband, father, mother, brother and sister are the nearest relatives and they get the first priority. If such near relatives do not exist, shares are given to the next nearest relatives. After the death of a man, therefore, his wealth is distributed amongst his kith and kin and a fatal blow is struck against the capitalistic concentration of wealth. This law of Islam is of unique excellence, and other societies are now taking similar action. But the sad irony is that Muslims themselves are not fully aware of its revolutionary potentialities and some of them, through ignorance, are even avoiding it in practice. In several parts of the Indo-Pakistan subcontinent daughters are being deprived of their share of inheritance; this is a palpable injustice and a flagrant violation of the Qur'ān's injunctions.

After the family and its connections come man's relations with his friends, neighbours, dwellers of his own locality, village or city, and persons with whom he comes into constant contact. Islam recognises these relations and enjoins a Muslim to treat them all honestly, truthfully, equitably and courteously. It bids believers to respect others' feelings, to avoid indecent and abusive language, to help each other, to attend to the sick, to support the destitute, to assist the needy and the crippled, to sympathise with the trouble-stricken, to look after orphans and widows, to feed the hungry, to clothe the under-clad and to help the unemployed in seeking employment.

Islam says that if God has bestowed upon you wealth and riches, do not squander it on luxurious frivolities. It has prohibited the use of gold and silver vessels, the wearing of costly silk dresses, and the wasting of money on useless ventures and extravagant luxuries. This injunction of the *Sharī'ah* is based on the principle that no man should be allowed to squander on himself wealth that could maintain thousands of human beings. It is cruel and unjust that money which can be used to feed teeming, starving humanity should be frittered away in useless ostentation. Islam does not want to deprive a man of his wealth and belongings. What one has earned or inherited is beyond doubt his own property. Islam recognises his right and allows him to enjoy it and make the best use of it. It also suggests that if you are wealthy, you should have better dress and good accommodation and a decent living. But Islam insists that the human element should not be lost sight of.

What Islam totally disapproves of is conceited self-centredness, which neglects the welfare and well-being of others and gives birth to an exaggerated individualism. It wants society as a whole to prosper, and not merely a few individuals. It instils in the minds of its followers social consciousness and suggests that they live a simple and frugal life, that they

111

avoid excesses and, while fulfilling their own needs, keep in mind the needs and requirements of their kith and kin, their near and distant relatives, their friends and associates, their neighbours and fellow-citizens.[7] This is what Islam wants to achieve.

So far we have discussed the nature of man's relations with his close relatives and friends. Now let us look at the wider perspective and see what kind of community Islam wants to establish. Everyone who embraces Islam not only enters the fold of the religion but also becomes a member of the Islamic community. The *Shari'ah* has formulated certain rules of behaviour for this as well. These rules oblige Muslims to help each other, to approve good and forbid evil, and to see that no wrong enters their society. Some of the injunctions of the law of Islam, in this respect, are as follows:

1. To preserve the moral life of the nation and to safeguard the evolution of society on healthy lines, free mingling of the sexes has been prohibited. Islam effects a functional distribution between the sexes and sets different spheres of activity for both of them. Women should in the main devote themselves to household duties in their homes and men should attend to their jobs in the socio-economic spheres. Outside the pale of the nearest relations between whom marriage is forbidden men and women have been asked not to mix freely with each other and if they do have to have contact with each other they should do so with *purdah*. When women have to go out of their homes, they should wear simple dress and be properly veiled. They should also cover their faces and hands as a normal course. Only in genuine necessity can they unveil, and they must re-cover as soon as possible.

Along with this, men have been asked to keep down their eyes and not to look at women. And if someone accidentally looks upon some woman, he should turn away his eyes. To try to see them is wrong and to try to seek their acquaintance is worse. It is the duty of both men and women to look after their personal morality and purge their souls of all impurities. Marriage is the proper form of sexual relationship and no-one should attempt to overstep this limit or even think of any sexual licence; the very thought and imagination of man should be purified from such perverse ideas.

2. For the same purpose it has been enjoined that proper dress should always be worn. No man should expose his body from the knees to the

---

7. The Qur'ăn says: "In their wealth the needy, the beggar, and the destitute have their due." (li, 19). *—Editor*

navel, nor should a woman expose any part of her body except her face and hands to any person other than her husband, however closely related to her he might be. This is technically called *satr* (cover) and to keep these parts covered is the religious duty of every man and woman. Through this directive Islam aims to cultivate in its followers a deep sense of modesty and purity and to suppress all forms of immodesty and moral deviation.

3. Islam does not approve of pastimes, entertainments and recreations which tend to stimulate sensual passions and vitiate the canons of morality. They are a sheer waste of time, money and energy, and destroy the moral fibre of society. Recreation in itself is certainly a necessity. It acts as a spur to activity and quickens the spirit of life and adventure. It is as important to life as water and air; one particularly requires rest and recreation after hard work. But it must be recreation which refreshes the mind and enlivens the spirit, and must not depress the spirit and deprave the passions. Absurd and wasteful entertainments wherein thousands of people witness depraving scenes of crime and immorality are the very antithesis of healthy recreation. Although they may be gratifying to the senses, their effect upon the minds and morals is horrifying. They can have no place in an Islamic society and culture.

4. To safeguard the unity and solidarity of the nation and to achieve the welfare and well-being of the Muslim community, believers have been enjoined to avoid mutual hostility, social dissensions and sectarianism of all kinds. They have been exhorted to settle their differences and disputes in accordance with the principles laid down in the Qur'ān and the *Sunnah,* and if the parties fail to reach a settlement, instead of fighting and quarrelling amongst themselves, they should bury their differences in the name of Allah and leave the decision to Him. In matters of common national welfare they should help each other, obey their leaders, and avoid wasting their energies in bickering over trivial things. Such feuds and schisms are a disgrace to the Muslim community and a potential source of national weakness. They must be shunned at all costs.

5. Islam regards knowledge and science as the common heritage of mankind and Muslims have absolute liberty to learn them and their practical uses from whatever source they can. But as far as the question of culture and the way of life is concerned, it forbids them to imitate the modes of living of other peoples. The psychology of imitation suggests that it springs from a sense of inferiority and abasement and its net result is the cultivation of a defeatist mentality. Cultural aping of others has

disastrous consequences on a nation; it destroys its inner vitality, blurs its vision, befogs its critical faculties, breeds an inferiority complex and gradually but assuredly saps all the springs of culture and sounds its death-knell.

This is why the Holy Prophet (blessings of Allah and peace be upon him) has positively and forcefully forbidden Muslims to assume the culture and mode of life of non-Muslims. The strength of a nation does not lie in its dress, etiquette or fine arts; its power and growth owe themselves to right knowledge, science, discipline, organisation and energy for action. If you want to learn from others, take lessons from their will to action and social discipline, avail yourselves of their knowledge and technical accomplishments but do not lean towards those arts and crafts which breed cultural slavery and national inferiority. Muslims have been enjoined to guard against such influence.

Now we come to the relationship of Muslims with non-Muslims. In dealing with them, believers have been instructed not to be intolerant or narrow-minded. They have been commanded not to abuse or speak ill of their religious leaders or saints, nor to say anything insulting about their religion. They have been instructed not to seek disputes with them unnecessarily but to live in peace and amity. If the non-Muslims observe peace and conciliatory attitudes towards Muslims, and do not violate their territories and other rights, they also should keep congenial and friendly relations with them and deal with them fairly and justly.

It is the very dictate of our religion that we possess greater human sympathy and politeness than any other people, and behave in most noble and modest ways. Bad manners, ill-behaviour, oppression and narrow-mindedness are against the very spirit of Islam. A Muslim is born in the world to become a living symbol of goodness, nobility and humanity. He should win the hearts of people by his character and example. Then alone he can become a true ambassador of Islam.

4. The Rights of All Creatures
Now we come to the last kind of rights. God has honoured man with authority over His countless creatures. Everything has been harnessed for him. He has been endowed with the power to subdue them and make them serve his objectives. This superior position gives man authority over them and he enjoys the right to use them as he likes. But that does not mean that God has given him unbridled liberty. Islam says that all creation has certain rights on man. They are: he should not waste them on fruitless

114

ventures nor should he unnecessarily hurt them or harm them. When he uses them for his service he should cause them the least possible harm, and should employ the best and the least injurious methods of using them.

The law of Islam embodies many injunctions about these rights. For instance, we are allowed to slaughter animals for food but have been forbidden to kill them merely for fun or sport. To slaughter them, the method of *dhabḥ* (slaughtering) has been fixed, the best possible method of obtaining meat from animals. Other methods are either more painful or spoil the meat and deprive it of some of its useful properties. Similarly, killing an animal by causing continuous pain and injury is considered abominable in Islam. Islam allows the killing of dangerous and venomous animals and of beasts of prey only because it values man's life more than theirs. But here, too, it does not allow their killing by resort to prolonged painful methods.

Regarding the beasts of burden and animals used for riding and transport, Islam distinctly forbids man to keep them hungry, to put intolerable burdens on them and to beat them cruelly. To catch birds and imprison them in cages without any special purpose is considered abominable. Islam does not approve even of the useless cutting of trees and bushes. Man can use their fruits and other produce, but he has not the right to destroy them. Vegetables, after all, possess life. Nor does Islam allow waste among even lifeless things; so much so that it disapproves of the wasteful flow of too much water. Its avowed purpose is to avoid waste in every conceivable form and to make the best use of all resources — living and lifeless.

Shari'ah — The Universal and Eternal Law

In the foregoing pages we have given a very brief *resumé* of the law of Islam — the law which Prophet Muḥammad (blessings of Allah and peace be upon him) delivered to mankind for all times to come. This law admits of no difference between man and man except in faith and religion. Those religious and social systems and political and cultural ideologies which differentiate between men on grounds of race, country or colour can never become universal creeds or world ideologies for the simple reason that someone belonging to a certain race cannot be transformed into another race, one born in a certain country cannot tear his identity from that place, nor can the whole world condense into one country; the colour of a negro, a Chinese and a white man cannot be changed. Such ideologies and social systems must remain confined to one race, country or community. They are bound to be narrow, limited and nationalistic. Islam, on the other hand, is a universal ideology. Any person who declares belief in *Lā ilāha illallāh*

115

Muḥammad-ur-Rasūlullāh (there is no other god worthy of worship than Allah, and Muḥammad is His Prophet) enters the pale of Islam and entitles himself to the same rights as those of other Muslims. Islam makes no discrimination on the basis of race, country, colour, language or the like. Its appeal is to the whole of humanity.

Its law is also eternal. It is not based on the customs or traditions of any particular people and is not meant for any particular period of human history. It is based on the same principles of nature on which man has been created. And as that nature remains the same in all periods and under all circumstances, law based on it is applicable to every period and under all circumstances.

This universal and eternal religion is *Islam*.